COLLECTING BOTTLES FOR FUN & PROFIT

William C. Ketchum, Jr.

HPBooks ®

Publisher: Rick Bailey
Editorial Director: Randy Summerlin
Editor: Jacqueline Sharkey
Art Director: Don Burton
Book Manufacture: Anthony B. Narducci
Typography: Cindy Coatsworth, Michelle Claridge

Published by HPBooks, Inc.
P.O. Box 5367
Tucson, AZ 85703
602-888-2150
ISBN: 0-89586-251-4
Library of Congress
   Catalog Card Number: 84-62579
©1985 HPBooks, Inc.
Printed in U.S.A.
1st Printing

Prepared for HPBooks by Sophia Books/Layla Productions, Inc.
Publisher: Carol Paradis
Designer: Allan Mogel

The author would like to thank the following who lent assistance
and permission to make photographs for this book:

Meryl Berman
Bottles Unlimited, New York, New York
Jay Hyams
Debra Lumpe
Eric Marshall
Jordan Meschcow
Sophie Paradis
Burton Spiller, Rochester, New York

All photos by Chun Lai, except for the following:
John Garetti—pages 5, 8 left, 9, 10, 31 top right, 61, 63, 66, 87 bottom, 88.
Calabro Studio—cover, pages 7 top left, 8 right, 15, 65, 69.

COLLECTING BOTTLES FOR FUN & PROFIT

William C. Ketchum, Jr.

Getting Started

If you collect bottles, you're not alone! More than three million Americans collect bottles, and the number is increasing. Bottles are America's third most popular collectible, following coins and stamps.

WHY IT'S POPULAR

Bottle-collecting is popular for many reasons. Like other antiques and collectibles, bottles are interesting because they tell us about our past. Even bottles made during this century are fascinating representatives of America's changing lifestyle. Bottles that have labels or imprints are of special interest to collectors of advertising memorabilia.

Bottles are attractive, too. Their many shapes, designs and colors make them ideal decorations for your home.

The greatest appeal of bottles is that they are plentiful and inexpensive. You don't need a fortune to assemble an enjoyable collection. Even with little money, you can hope to make a *find*—a valuable bottle at a low price. In addition, many collectible bottles are a good investment, increasing in value every year.

Bottle collecting may be the most democratic American hobby. It is one pastime in which everyone— rich, poor, young or old alike—can participate. It's a hobby that the entire family can enjoy without spending much money. Many valuable and interesting bottles can be found in attics or at flea markets. Building a collection can be a wonderful treasure hunt for everyone.

With a little money, you can enter the exciting world of bottle shops and auctions. If you know what to look for, you may discover a valuable bottle others have overlooked.

ACQUIRING BOTTLES IS EASY

Beginning collectors and seasoned veterans are faced with the same abundance of bottles. Millions were made in the United States and Canada during the past 200 years. Countless others were imported. Most of these bottles were made quickly and sold inexpensively. They originally held different kinds of liquids, such as liquor, medicine, perfume and poison. When they were empty, many of these containers were thrown away. However, many others were saved. Thrifty people used them to store other liquids or sold them to the junkman.

Often, bottles were thrown away into dumps or old wells. Bottles saved were put in closets, attics or basements. In these ways, thousands of early bottles were preserved.

When you go looking for collectible bottles, you won't have to worry about not finding any. You're lucky! Collectors of other items, such as porcelain, silver and furniture, must contend with small quantities and high prices. You'll find plenty of bottles to choose among. And, many are free. All you really need to start your collection is a shovel to dig with.

Although plenty of bottles are available, some types and specific bottles are difficult to find. Certain bottles have become favorites with collectors, and the prices for these can be quite high. For example, *historical flasks* are very popular. These are small, flattened whiskey bottles decorated with embossed figures of historical characters or patriotic symbols. Even the most ordinary historical flask may cost $50. One-of-a-kind historical flasks in excellent condition have sold for as much as $25,000. Canning jars, such as the familiar Mason jars, are usually inexpensive. However, don't be surprised if you come across a rare example selling for over $1,000.

HOW THIS BOOK HELPS

How can you determine whether a bottle is just an ordinary example or is a rare and valuable specimen? The only way is to learn how to identify, date and evaluate the bottles you come across. This book will give you the necessary information.

This book provides a brief guide to all the major bottle types. The bottles are categorized by original contents. Illustrations show the most common and some of the rare forms. A price guide keyed to the illustrations enables you to tell at a glance the value of the bottle shown. The book includes information on building a collection and researching your collection. Because many collectors buy and sell bottles, you'll learn about that, too. Most important, the book contains plenty of advice and ideas on how to find bottles. Whether in an attic or at a local flea market, the bottles you want are available. Good luck, and have fun!

Chestnut bottles, such as the ones above, were among the first American
bottles and are extremely popular with present-day collectors.

Glossary

The following terms are used throughout this book. This glossary will help you understand the world of bottle collecting.

Applied decoration—Small, decorative bits of glass affixed to a bottle after it is expanded or removed from its mold.

Applied decoration: Designs were added to the bottle after it was made.

Art glass—Decorative colored glass that is usually hand-formed. Most art glass can be found in the form of vases and other fancy glassware.

Attached—Glassmakers use this term to describe something joined to a bottle.

Bail closure—A stopper consisting of a porcelain, glass or metal top and a piece of wire wrapped around the bottle neck. The stopper clamps over the top of the bottle. Used on beer bottles, soda bottles and canning jars.

Batch—Glassmakers' term for the mixture of ingredients from which glass is made.

Bitters—A type of patent medicine, usually consisting of a mixture of water, bitter herbs, a coloring agent and

Bail closure: This type of hinged closure is still in use.

a substantial amount of alcohol.

Black glass—See *green glass*.

Blob top—The thick, doughnut-shaped rim, or top, used primarily on soda-water, mineral-water and beer bottles.

Blowpipe—Hollow iron tube, 2 to 6 feet long, used by glassblowers. The worker blows air through the pipe to expand a glob of hot glass.

Calabash—Gourd-shaped whiskey flask of the 1850s,

Blob top: A type of rim that often appeared on soda and mineral-water bottles.

with a long neck and bulbous sides. (See page 37.)

Candy-stripe glass — Type of art glass consisting of thin strands of white against contrasting background. Sometimes used for barber bottles.

Carnival glass — Iridescent pressed glass. Popular colors include orange, purple and green.

Closure — A device used to seal bottles. Corks, caps and stoppers are all closures. Made of various materials, including glass, metal, rubber, porcelain and cork.

Crown cork — Metal cap with cork liner, used to seal beer and soda bottles. Also known as *crown cap*.

Crucible — Large clay pot in which the ingredients of a batch of glass are placed. The crucible is placed in an oven, where the batch melts.

Decolorizing — Process of adding materials such as manganese or arsenic to a batch of glass to make it colorless.

Embossing: Decorations embossed on a bottle can include pictures and advertising material.

Bitters: More than 1,000 varieties of bitters bottles are available.

Enameling: The top portion of this bottle was painted with enamels after the bottle was completed.

These materials remove or neutralize the natural iron impurities that make bottle glass green, amber or aqua.

Dip mold — Simple one-piece mold, open at the top and usually set in the floor of a glass factory. It is used to form the lower body of a bottle. A hot glob of glass on the end of a blowpipe is inserted in the mold. When the glassmaker blows through the pipe, the glass expands until it takes the shape of the mold. The formed bottle is simply lifted up through the open top.

Embossing — Raised decoration, usually words or figures, on the surface of a bottle.

Enameling — Decorating a bottle by painting it with enamels. When painting is completed, the enamels are fixed by refiring the bottle at a low temperature. Barber bottles are often decorated with enamels.

European figurals — Bottles inspired by the technical quality and intricate designs of European glassmakers. Bottles often depict political personalities and sports heroes. These bottles originally contained imported liquors or brandies.

Figurals — Bottles shaped like human figures, animals, buildings and varied objects.

Finish — Collectors' term for the last step in making a bottle, when the neck and lip are formed.

Fire polishing — Reheating a completed bottle to smooth its surface and remove tool marks.

Flask — Small, flattened, oval whiskey bottle.

Free-blown bottles — Bottles formed by blowing

through a blowpipe. Such bottles are shaped by hand, without the use of molds. (See pages 13-14.)

Full mold—A mold that produces a full-sized bottle. Bottles made in a full mold do not need to be expanded further when they are removed from the mold.

Gather—Glassmakers' term for a blob of hot glass picked up on the end of a blowpipe. As the glassmaker blows air through the pipe, the gather is expanded to form a bottle.

Glass press—A manufacturing device that worked like a waffle iron. A glob of hot glass was deposited in the press. The top was closed and the piece was formed in the press. Few of today's collectibles were made this way.

Green glass—Common bottle glass. The shades of green vary from dark green (also called *black glass)* to aqua. The colors result from iron impurities in the sand from which the glass is made.

Hand-blown—Bottles that are shaped by blowing and sometimes with the use of molds, but without the use of automatic bottle-making machines.

Historical flasks—Usually small, flattened, egg-shaped whiskey bottles decorated with embossed figures of historical characters or patriotic symbols. Common figures include George Washington, John Quincy Adams, Lafayette, the American flag and the American bald eagle.

Historical flasks: Eagles were among the popular historical symbols embossed on flasks. These historical flasks were common in the late 18th and early 19th centuries.

Hobnail glass—Type of art glass covered with a knob-like pattern. Sometimes used for barber bottles.

Hutchinson device—Stopper that was partially inserted into a bottle and worked like a plunger. Used primarily on soda-water and beer bottles from 1879 to 1891.

Kick-up—Rounded indentation in the base of a bottle. Kick-ups are common on wine and champagne bottles.

Marver—Smooth stone slab used in making free-blown bottles. The gather of molten glass was rolled on the marver. This ensured that the bottle would have uniform thickness.

Masonic flask—Flask that bears the symbols of the Masonic society, an extremely powerful political group during the early 19th century.

Metal—Glassmakers' term for the batch, after it has become liquid.

Milk glass—Opaque glass that is usually white, but is sometimes made in blue.

Mold—Metal, pottery or wooden form into which molten glass is poured. The glass is then expanded and takes the shape and design of the mold.

Mold mark—Ridge left on the surface of a bottle formed in a mold. This mark occurs because the two parts of a mold never fit together precisely. When the mold is closed, molten glass is forced between the cracks, creating ridges on the finished piece. Also called *seam.*

Name plate—A piece of paper carrying the names or initials of the original owners of barber bottles. The paper was placed behind a piece of clear glass attached to the bottle.

Neck—The narrow upper portion of a bottle, terminating in the rim or lip.

Paper label—Printed label on a bottle, describing its contents.

Patent medicine—Medicine whose name was registered as a trademark. Also called *proprietary medicine.*

Pictorial flask—Whiskey flask embossed with scenes, or with objects such as ships, trains, trees, houses or animals.

Piece mold—Mold made in two or three parts that are hinged together.

Pitkin bottle—Flask made in the late 18th or early 19th centuries by the Pitkin Glass Works in East Hartford, Connecticut.

Plate mold—Mold that has a hole cut into one side, to allow insertion of various pieces of metal called *slug plates.* Each slug plate can be embossed with the name of a merchant or manufacturer. In this way, the same mold can be used to make bottles for several different companies.

Pontil mark—Scar left on the base of a bottle when a *pontil rod* is drawn away from the bottle. Early pontil rods, used until 1845, left a rough, circular mark called an *open pontil.* Pontil rods used from 1845 to 1860 left a

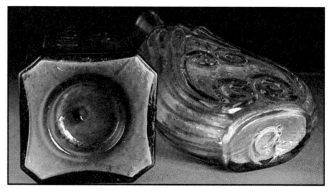

Iron pontil: Learn to recognize pontil marks. They help date a bottle. (See pages 13-15.)

smooth, round indentation called an *iron pontil* or *improved pontil*.

Pontil rod—Long, usually solid, iron rod. Used to hold the bottom of a bottle while the upper portions, such as neck and rim, were being finished.

Proprietary medicine—Another name for patent medicine.

Sampler—Small, figural whiskey bottle containing whiskey sample. Also called *tasters,* these bottles were given away by tavern owners and liquor dealers.

Scroll flask—Pear-shaped whiskey bottle that came in several sizes, ranging from half-pint to one gallon. Also called *violin flask.*

Seal bottle—Vessel bearing a lump of glass, like a blob of sealing wax, imprinted with the name or initials of a manufacturer or owner.

Seam—Another name for mold mark.

Shoulder—The sloping sides of a bottle just below the neck.

Show bottle—Drug bottle made with artificially colored glass.

Sick glass—Collectors' term for glass that has turned white or iridescent because of long exposure to water or dampness. Condition is irreversible. (See page 62.)

Slug plate—See *plate mold.*

Snap case—Clothespin-shaped metal cradle used to hold bottles while their necks and rims were being completed. Introduced about 1850, the snap case was used until automatic bottle-making machines were developed. A bottle held in a snap case had no pontil mark.

Sunburst flask—Flask having square shoulders, embossed with a large motif consisting of rays extending from a central point. The sunburst was a common motif in the Federal period of the late 18th and early 19th centuries.

Sun-colored glass—Collectors' term for glass that was originally clear but has taken on an amethyst or purple tint. These colors result from the sun's ultraviolet rays reacting with the manganese in the glass. (Manganese was added to the glass to decolorize it.) Sun-colored glass is especially prized by collectors in the western United States.

Target ball—Small, hollow, glass sphere used for shooting practice in the middle to late 19th century.

Taster—Another name for *sampler.*

Three-piece mold—Common 19th-century mold made of three parts, hinged together. After a bottle had been expanded in this mold, the mold could be opened for removal of the bottle.

Torpedo—Soda-water bottle shaped like a torpedo. Because of its narrow bottom, this bottle had to be placed on its side.

Turn-mold bottle—Collectors' term for bottle that has been polished and has had its mold marks removed. The latter was achieved by spinning the bottle in the

Sunburst flasks: Many bottles used a sunburst motif. It also appears on furniture and other objects from the Federal period during the late 19th and early 20th centuries.

mold before extraction. This was a common practice with certain types of bottles, particularly late 19th-century wine bottles.

Vasa murrhina—Type of varicolored art glass with metallic silver or gold flecks. Sometimes used for barber bottles.

Violin flask—See *scroll flask.*

Wax sealer—Canning jar first made in the 1820s. The jar was sealed by pouring hot wax over the top of the contents and applying a tin or cork lid.

Whittle marks—Dimpled or wavy marks on the surfaces of some molded bottles. Whittle marks were originally thought to have been formed by the whittled inside surfaces of wooden molds. They are now known to have been caused by contractions in the glass resulting from blowing hot glass into cold metal molds.

The Story of American Bottles

Before you begin collecting bottles, you should know about the history of bottle making. You should also know how bottles are made. This information will help you identify the many bottles you encounter.

EARLY AMERICAN BOTTLES

Although the earliest settlers in this country set up glassmaking shops, their efforts were seldom successful. Unlike most crafts important to the early Americans, glassmaking required skilled workers who understood complex chemical formulas. It also required various raw materials, including enormous quantities of wood to fuel the furnaces.

Training workers and acquiring raw materials required money and government cooperation. Both were lacking in America during its early years. The English authorities discouraged such activities. They wanted the colonists to buy English products—including glass. They wanted the colonists to provide England with raw materials. This situation, of course, was one of the causes of the American Revolution.

FIRST AMERICAN GLASS FACTORY

Even though the English tried to prevent it, some glass factories were established in America. A German named Caspar Wistar built a glassworks in Salem County, New Jersey, in 1738. It was probably America's first profitable glass factory. Wistar made many kinds of glass items, including bottles.

Other important early American glass factories included those run by Henry William Stiegel and John Frederick Amelung. These factories produced a great deal of glass, but both factories eventually went bankrupt.

Don't look for bottles made in these early glass factories. Few specimens exist. Those that do cost more than most collectors are willing to pay.

START OF THE BOTTLE-MAKING INDUSTRY

Most early glassmakers were located in the East, particularly in New England. By the end of the 18th century, Americans—and American glassmakers—had begun to move west. You will probably read or hear about a category of glass called *Pittsburgh glass.* It was called this because many glassmakers lived and worked in Pittsburgh.

The period from about 1820 to about 1880 is particularly important. During this time the industry firmly established itself, with important factories in New England and the Midwest.

The first products of these factories were storage bottles made with green glass. During the 1820s, many factories began to make historical flasks. These factories also made containers for bitters and other medicines. Toward the end of this period, new and now highly collectible types of containers appeared. These included barber, canning and most food-storage jars.

Among the earliest and most interesting American bottles are the Pitkin flasks.
These were produced in Connecticut during the early 19th century.

CANADIAN BOTTLES

It took even longer for the Canadian bottle-making industry to get started. It was not until the mid-19th century that a few small factories opened.

However, many factories in the United States, especially in New York and New Hampshire, provided bottles for Canadian products. Because these are marked with the names of the Canadian companies that used them, it is usually not possible to know that they were not made in Canada.

IDENTIFYING OLD BOTTLES

Many small glass factories operated during the 19th and early 20th centuries. Most have disappeared. The few that have survived are part of the large glass industry established at the end of the 1800s. Very few of these early shops marked their products. Those that did marked only a fraction of their bottles. Therefore, it is difficult to determine where a particular old bottle was made.

The methods used to identify an old bottle are somewhat like detective work. Sometimes, you can identify a bottle by comparing it to advertisements in old newspapers. Or, an old bottle may resemble bottles known to have been made at a certain factory.

Although it may be difficult to identify, an old

bottle may be a beautiful and tangible reminder of one of America's earliest and most important crafts.

HOW GLASS IS MADE

All collectible bottles are made with glass. Glassmaking is an art more than 2,000 years old. Over the centuries, there have been many changes in the ways bottles have been made and decorated. However, the ingredients used to make glass are still the same.

INGREDIENTS

All glass is made from a combination of two elements. The first is silica, which is usually obtained from sand. The second is an alkali, such as lime, potash or carbonate of soda.

Other ingredients are sometimes added to control the color of the glass. Aqua, green or amber tints may result from impurities in the sand. To avoid these tints, glassmakers sometimes add a *decolorant* to the mixture. To create new colors, glassmakers add metallic compounds, such as cobalt, which produces blue.

All ingredients must be mixed together in correct proportions. The special formulas for these mixtures are complicated. Many are closely guarded secrets.

Glassmakers call this mixture of ingredients a *batch*. The batch is placed in a large pot—or *crucible*—made of clay. The crucible is placed in an oven. Some ovens hold only one crucible. Others may hold several dozen. The batch is heated at high temperatures until the ingredients melt, forming a thick, sticky substance that can be shaped.

OVENS

The earliest and simplest ovens were rectangular, with open fire pits. These ovens were used for at least 1,000 years. They were replaced in the 17th century by round ovens with two chambers. The lower one was a firebox. The upper one was the heating chamber that held the crucible. All ovens were originally wood-fired, but coal and gas were used later on.

In the 19th century, a more efficient oven, shaped like a beehive, came into use. This oven had three chambers, one atop the other. At the bottom was the fire pit. In the center was a heating chamber. At the top was an annealing oven, in which finished glassware was placed to allow it to cool slowly. This was important because sudden cooling could crack the glass.

The crucible containing the batch of glassmaking ingredients was left in the oven for 30 to 40 hours. As

In this early 19th-century illustration, we can see bottlemakers at work in a factory. Note the various steps in the bottlemaking process.

the ingredients melted, workmen removed the impurities, which floated to the surface. When the batch became liquid—called *metal*—it was allowed to cool. When it had thickened slightly, it was ready to be worked.

FORMING BOTTLES

The earliest American bottles were formed by a process known as *free-blowing*. This technique had been used for centuries in Europe and the Near East. It involved the use of a blowpipe—a hollow iron rod that was 2 to 6 feet long.

The blowpipe was inserted into the oven through a small opening. A glob of the molten glass—called a *gather*—would stick to the end of the blowpipe. The gather was rolled back and forth on a smooth stone slab called a *marver*. The rolling created an even surface, which ensured that the glass, when expanded, would have a uniform thickness. Then the glassblower would insert the other end of the pipe in his mouth and blow through it.

As air entered the gather, the glass expanded, much like a balloon. As the glassblower worked, he turned or twirled the pipe so the glass maintained a symmetrical shape. Because the gather could only be shaped while it was hot, it was often necessary to put it back into the oven for a moment.

Several other steps were involved in forming the glass vessel. It was spun in a round wooden bowl to keep the sides symmetrical. It was rubbed back and forth across a block of wood, to flatten the bottom. It was pulled by a pincer-shaped tool to elongate the neck.

Finally, the rim or lip was formed. The worker attached a small glob of hot glass to another iron rod, called a *pontil rod*. This device was shorter than the blowpipe and was solid. The hot glass on the end of the pontil was pressed against the bottom of the bottle. This attached the bottle to the pontil rod. The neck of the bottle could then be separated from the blowpipe. To do this, the worker simply applied a drop of water to the top edge of the bottle. This caused the hot glass to crack. The bottle was then put back into the oven to make the glass at the neck soft. The soft glass was reshaped with shears and a special lipping device.

The final step was to break the bottle off the pontil rod. This left a circular, rough-edged scar on the base of the bottle. This was called a *pontil mark* or an *open-pontil mark*. As you will see, this mark is of great importance in dating bottles.

FREE-BLOWN BOTTLES

You can recognize many free-blown bottles by their balloonlike shape and their lack of surface decoration. They are also often slightly lopsided. Not all free-blown bottles were round, however. It was possible to make the body square or oval. Some common types,

The Pitkin flask, made between 1810 and 1840, was among the earliest American flasks. Most held less than a quart. They were made with dark green or amber glass and were pontil-marked.

such as early case-gin bottles, come in these shapes.

The colors you are most likely to find are aqua, dark green—sometimes called *black*—and amber. Early glass factories produced these colors because they were the most inexpensive.

Free-blown bottles had their drawbacks. Their walls, stretched thin by expansion, were fragile. Moreover, it took a relatively long time to make each bottle—usually 5 to 7 minutes. A faster process existed. In pre-Christian times, the Egyptians and Syrians had used hollow molds to shape their vessels. This technique was later employed by American glassworks.

MOLDS

The earliest molds used by American glassmakers were called *dip molds.* These cuplike receptacles were often set into the factory floor. They were used to form the lower body of the bottle. The glassblower inserted the gather into the mold, expanded it and then withdrew it. Such molds were intended primarily to form the glass, not to decorate it. However, designs cut into the sides of some molds left a corresponding raised pattern on the expanded vessel.

Piece molds were more sophisticated. They were made in two or three parts hinged together. These molds could be used to shape the entire bottle, except for the upper neck and lip. The gather was inserted into the mold, the parts were closed, and the gather was expanded. The blowpipe was taken out, and the neck finished. Then the mold was opened and a fully formed bottle removed.

Mold-formed bottles had great commercial advantages over free-blown bottles. They could be made much more rapidly and uniformly.

In addition, the bottles could serve as advertisements. The name of a product and its manufacturer's name and address could be cut into a mold. Making an endless number of identical bottles was possible, each acting as an advertisement for the product it contained.

By the 1870s, the process had become even more refined. Plate molds were created. These molds had special openings into which metal disks—called *slug plates*—could be inserted. Each disk was embossed with the name of a different product. The same mold could be used for bottles intended for several different companies.

The development of molds corresponded to the rise of the patent-medicine industry. Hundreds of thousands of medicine bottles had embossed names along with the usual paper label. Because so many of these bottles still exist, they are very popular with collectors.

IMPROVED PONTIL

At the same time that molds were being improved, other developments changed the bottle-making industry. About 1845, some manufacturers did away with the traditional pontil rod and its glob of hot glass. They used a rod that had a flaring lip. When this lip was heated red-hot, it adhered to the bottom of a bottle.

This device—called an *iron,* or *improved, pontil*—was used until about 1860. You can recognize a bottle made this way by the dark, circular impression on its base. You may spot tiny flecks of iron oxide (rust) in this impression. Called an *iron-pontil mark,* it is most often found on soda, mineral and beer bottles.

In this illustration, we can see a glassmaker applying the handle to a pitcher. Handles were applied in a similar manner to whiskey bottles.

SNAP CASE

An even more efficient device for holding a bottle while the neck was shaped was invented about 1850. This was the *snap case,* a Y-shaped iron rod with cuplike grips set between the open ends.

A workman placed a bottle between the grips. He then moved an iron ring down the handle of the snap case. The ring was attached to the grips. Its movements forced the grips to close around the bottle.

The snap-case method was faster and easier than previous methods. And, it left the bottom of the bottle smooth and unmarked. By 1870, all American bottles were being made with the snap-case method.

INNOVATIONS IN BOTTLE MAKING

Bottles made in molds had advantages, but they also had problems. For instance, they had mold marks, also called *seams.* The different parts of a mold never fit together precisely. When the mold was closed over hot glass, some of the glass squeezed between the cracks. This resulted in tiny ridges on the finished piece.

Some manufacturers cut their molds so the seams blended with the decorative design of the bottle. This was particularly common with historical flasks. Other manufacturers, especially the producers of wine bottles, removed the marks. They coated the inside of the mold with a thick paste. Before removing the bottle from the mold, they would spin the bottle, wiping away the seams. Naturally, these *turn-mold* bottles had to be round. Most date from 1880 to 1900.

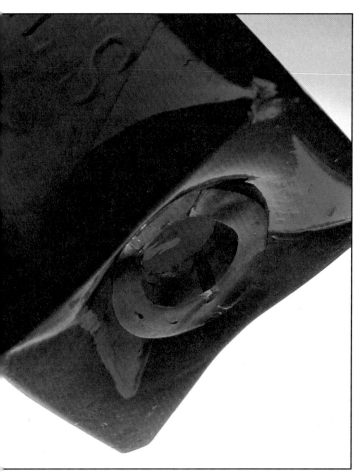

Look for these marks to help you determine a bottle's age. A large, open-pontil mark with rough edges, like the one on this bottle, is characteristic of pieces made before 1845. Sharp edges were created when the bottle was broken free from the pontil rod.

A shallow depression, covered with black or dirty-white material, is characteristic of bottles on which an iron pontil was used. Bottles made from about 1845 to 1860 were frequently marked this way.

Another major problem facing bottle makers was the time it took to mold each bottle. Manufacturers needed a machine to speed up the process. In 1903, the Owens Bottle Machine Co. provided just that. Their machine did everything from shaping the molten glass to cooling the finished bottle—jobs formerly done by skilled craftsmen. By 1912, the Owens machine was in use throughout the United States. Essentially, this put the skilled, commercial glassblower out of business. Canadian makers were slower to adopt the new machines, and as late as 1920 they were still employing glassblowers.

Machine-blown bottles are easy to distinguish from their free-blown counterparts. Machine-blown bottles always have a thin seam running over the lip. Such a seam could not have been created by even the best molds for free-blown bottles. Those molds required some part of the lip of the bottle to be reheated and shaped by hand. Therefore, free-blown bottles lack that one telltale seam. This seam is one of the first things you should look for when you are evaluating a bottle.

Until quite recently, collectors showed little interest in machine-made bottles. However, many enthusiasts are beginning to recognize that machine-made bottles have many appealing characteristics. They come in attractive colors and shapes. Many are more than 60 years old. Best of all, these bottles are plentiful and inexpensive.

GLASS PRESS

The glass press was one innovation that was not used to manufacture most bottles that interest collectors. First patented in 1825 by the Pittsburgh firm of Bakewell and Page, the press was an extremely simple device that worked like a waffle iron. A glob of hot glass was dropped onto the bottom of the press. The top was closed. And the piece was formed.

Glass presses were first used for such items as doorknobs. Eventually, they were used to manufacture glass tableware. Few collectible bottles were produced this way. However, the thin glass tops used on some early Mason and other canning jars were made in glass presses.

You now know how bottles are made. You can probably appreciate the skill and effort that went into the process. Best of all, you have the necessary information to identify and date most of the bottles you will obtain.

Remember that most bottles made before 1845 have rough, open-pontil marks. Bottles from 1845 to 1860 may have either iron-pontil marks or no marks. Bottles made after 1860 are usually unmarked. There are exceptions, of course, but these are the general guidelines.

Bottle Categories

Bottles come in many different shapes, sizes and colors. In addition, they've been used many different ways. The first step in becoming a bottle collector is to learn how to recognize the different types of bottles. The easiest way to do this is to categorize bottles by their original contents. You will see that the various shapes, sizes and colors of bottles usually reflect these original contents.

The bottles discussed and illustrated in this book are categorized this way. This book covers the major categories used by collectors throughout America. Each chapter covers a different category, and you will learn to recognize bottles according to what they originally contained.

There are hundreds—even thousands—of different bottles within each category. To give you a clear idea of how to recognize the different types, this book discusses common and rare forms. When you finish each chapter, you will know how to identify various kinds of bottles. And you will know whether a bottle is unusual or rare.

CHOOSING CATEGORIES

Before you begin a collection, you should decide how much money you want to spend. Certain categories of bottles, such as flasks, are expensive. Other categories, such as beer bottles and patent-medicine bottles, are so vast that the majority of the bottles available are quite inexpensive.

Don't be discouraged if you find yourself drawn to a high-priced category. There are always some bottles reasonably priced. If you're lucky, you may find an expensive bottle at a low price. You may even find a costly bottle in a dump or old house. One of the most wonderful aspects of bottle collecting is that it is like a treasure hunt. There is always the chance of making a big find—just when you least expect it!

Remember that some categories are much more popular than others. Prices for popular bottles are high, and competition for desirable specimens is intense. If you are just starting out, it is better to collect less-popular bottles. Rather than searching for expensive flasks, why not collect medicine or food bottles? This

way, you will find more bottles at much lower prices. You will also make your mistakes with less-expensive bottles. You can always trade or sell bottles later if you decide to change your collection.

Collect for the *fun* of it. Investment can be an important part of collecting bottles, but don't let it become too important. If you are constantly checking the value of your purchases, chances are you aren't really enjoying your hobby. The real joy of bottle collecting comes from sharing your collection with friends and family. Along the way, you'll also learn something about history and an important American industry.

It is not always clear what purpose a bottle served. These may be bitters bottles or whiskey bottles. These pineapple-shaped examples are pontiled and marked *W & Co., N.Y.*

Medicine bottles in various shades of green made between 1840 and 1880.
Left to right: Old Dr. Townsend's Sarsaparilla with iron-pontil mark; Pine Tree
Tar Cordial; Laboratory of C. W. Merchant, with iron-pontil mark.

PATENT-MEDICINE BOTTLES

Patent-medicine bottles will probably be the first bottles you encounter as a collector. More patent-medicine bottles are available than any other type, and they form the basis of most collections.

Why are there so many patent-medicine bottles? The answer is simple. At some point, all of our ancestors became ill. When they did, they turned to patent medicines.

PATENTS OF ROYAL FAVOR

The term *patent medicine* has an interesting history. It originally referred to the *patents of royal favor* issued by the king of England. The king granted these patents to the makers of certain medicines. The patent entitled the maker to a monopoly. That is, he was the only one allowed to sell the medicine. The maker also received other financial benefits.

You might suppose that if the king gave a special patent for a medicine, then the medicine had to be effective. This was not the case. Sometimes, getting a patent was the result of the manufacturer's social or political connections.

PATENTS IN AMERICA

As far as we know, royal patents were never issued for medicines made in America. Even so, when American factories began producing medicines, the makers frequently registered the name of their concoction as a trademark. They would then refer to the medicine as *patented*.

Few of these products were actually patented under American law. To do so would have required the maker to reveal the contents of the secret formula. Some makers did not want to do this because they believed their medicine contained curative ingredients. They didn't want competitors to find out about the contents. Most makers kept the contents of the medicines secret because they didn't want *anyone* to know what was in them. Most of these "medicines" were really little more than a mixture of water, flavoring and whiskey.

PROPRIETARY MEDICINES

Patent medicines are also referred to as *proprietary* medicines. The people who manufactured and sold the medicines were known as *proprietors,* or owners. You may call the bottles either *patent medicines* or *proprietary medicines.* They mean the same thing to most collectors.

The first patent medicines used in America were made in England and imported. They were packed in small, round or oval free-blown bottles and were identified by a paper label. These early bottles were marked with a pontil. You will find very few of these containers

Figural medicine bottles made between 1870 and 1880. Here are two examples of the Warner's Tippecanoe container, which is barrel-shaped and embossed with an Indian in a canoe. Few medicine bottles were decorated.

Dr. Guysott's Compound Extract of Yellow Dock & Sarsaparilla made between 1875 and 1890. Color is important in determining the value of medicine bottles. This bottle's rich green color makes it worth much more than the same bottle in aqua-colored glass.

Medicine bottle for Olmstead's Constitutional Beverage dates from the late 19th century. The yellow-green color of this bottle is unusual.

EMBOSSED BOTTLES

An *embossing* is decoration or letters that are above the surface of the bottle. The first known embossed American medicine bottle is the rather rare Dr. Robertson's Family Medicine, about 1810. The appearance of this category reflected the increasing competition in the patent-medicine industry.

Why Embossing Was Used—Embossing was a means of protecting makers from counterfeiters. A proprietor with a popular remedy soon found that other people were using his product's name. They would print copies of his labels—usually with some slight alteration in wording—and sell their medicines as his. Embossing a name on a bottle didn't stop counterfeiting, but did make it more difficult. With an embossed bottle, counterfeiters had to order a matching bottle, which was costly.

The introduction of embossed bottles reflected the emergence of medicines as a *growth industry*. Disease was commonplace. Even minor ailments, such as colds, flu or chicken pox, could end in death. Families faced with illness would pay dearly for relief.

Makers of patent medicines faced little competition from those who called themselves "doctors." Until the second half of the 19th century, medical training was rudimentary and licensing largely unknown. The origin of disease was not understood, and preventive methods, including sanitation, were generally not practiced. Doctors—who often called themselves *homeopathic, eclectic* or *botanic physicians*—often resorted to patent medicines. Usually, they could offer nothing better. Indeed, many patent medicines were developed by such doctors.

with labels intact. Even if you do find an old bottle with a label, you cannot be sure that the bottle was used in this country. Many medicine bottles were imported by 20th-century bottle dealers. Accordingly, most collectors have little interest in these early medicines.

Examples of pontil-marked patent medicine bottles made between 1830 and 1850. Left to right: C. W. Merchant, Chemist; Compound Balsam of Hoarhound; Amber Smith's Green Mountain Renovator; American Oil; Shaker Cherry Pectoral Syrup.

However, don't be fooled by the inclusion of the title *Doctor* in the name of a proprietary medicine. Use of the word did not mean that the maker *was* a doctor, even by 19th-century standards. Many makers simply assumed the name to improve sales. On the label of a patent medicine, anyone could claim to be a doctor.

By 1820, the American patent-medicine industry was fully developed. Between 1820 and 1910 at least 5,000 remedies were placed on the market. Because the majority were sold in embossed bottles, you can hope to collect a large assortment. The bottles made between 1810 and 1850 were pontil-marked. These are among the most popular and costly specimens.

Why They Are Popular—Embossed bottles are popular because of their age, rarity and hue. Many were blown with colored glass, including red, blue, deep green (an especially popular color) and yellow. Later bottles, made with the aid of the snap case, were almost always aqua, amber or clear.

Although medicine bottles may be expensive, they almost always cost much less than historical flasks or bitters bottles, discussed later. Medicines are therefore ideal for the young collector or the collector of modest means. You will be able to buy dozens of bottles for less than $10 each.

Like most collectors, you will probably be attracted to the unusual colors of some patent-medicine bottles. Don't expect to find medicine bottles in interesting forms, and don't look for attractive decoration. Flasks, whiskeys and even beer bottles have greater variations in form and decoration. Most of the medicines you will encounter will be square or rectangular. They have high, sloping shoulders and a relatively short neck. You may find some that are round or oval. You may even encounter some that are eight-sided. These will be the exceptions, however. Remember that the manufacturers of medicines were not selling a look—they were selling health.

PATENT-MEDICINE LABELS

The most important aspect of medicine bottles was the printed paper label. It contained the miraculous claims of the manufacturer for his product. Here is an example from the label of Clark Stanley's Snake Oil Liniment:

> "A wonderful pain destroying compound. The strongest and best liniment known for the cure of all pain and lameness. For rheumatism, neuralgia, sciatica, lame back, lumbago, contracted muscles, toothache, sprains, swellings, etc. Cures frost bite, chilblains, bruises, sore throat, bites of animals and insects and reptiles. (IS GOOD FOR EVERYTHING A LINIMENT SHOULD BE GOOD FOR.)"

This is not an extreme example of the advertising found on these bottles. Actually, it is relatively restrained. At least Clark did not claim to cure nonexistent complaints or incurable diseases of that time. The makers of many "medicines" offered no more than an illusion of hope to the sufferers who bought their products. With products such as Swift's Syphilitic Specific and Dr. J. Watson's Cancer and Scrofula Syrup, the claim on the label promised the impossible.

Regrettably, most medicine bottles have lost their original paper labels. The words embossed on the containers usually include only the name of the remedy and its manufacturer. The embossing gives just a hint of the wondrous claims that were printed on those bits of paper.

Every serious collector covets bottles with original labels. An even better find is a bottle with its label, plus the box in which it was packed and the crate in which it was shipped. The Log Cabin Extract bottle shown here is an example of such a treasure. It gives you an idea of what these medicine bottles looked like when store shelves were lined with them.

ADVERTISING

The claims on the labels were only part of the advertising for patent medicines. As early as the 18th century, medicine makers realized that advertising was crucial to their success. Before 1850, the bulk of advertising space in newspapers was taken by blurbs for these medicines. Manufacturers used a *hard sell,* not only because of the intense competition, but also because of the price of their wares. The standard cost per bottle in the late 19th century was $1—the equivalent of a day's wages!

The sellers of patent medicines also used other gimmicks. These included medicine shows, medicine men, posters, trade cards and giveaways.

THE MEDICINE MAN

The medicine man was an especially interesting feature of this business and appears in no other area of bottle sales. During the 19th century, most Americans and Canadians lived in the country or in small towns. The salesman, traveling around the various communities, was a common sight. Sometimes he sold only one medicine; sometimes he sold a variety of products.

The medicine man usually started his career as a *low-pitch man.* He walked, or traveled on public transportation, and carried his products in a suitcase or satchel. When he arrived in a town, he would climb on a box or a porch and deliver his *pitch.* A crowd would gather as he explained the wonders of the medicines he was selling. In this era, salesmen were expected to provide entertainment, so it was helpful if the medicine man could sing, play an instrument or do magic tricks.

Successful medicine men became *high-pitch men.*

Lydia E. Pinkham's Vegetable Compound bottle was made between 1875 and 1890. One of the easiest to find of all patent medicines, this bottle sells today for about what it cost when new and full!

It's difficult to find medicine bottles in good original condition. This Warner's Log Cabin Extract bottle is worth between $40 and $50. If it had its original label and contents, it would be worth $100 to $130. With its cardboard container and the original wooden packing box, the bottle is valued at about $225 to $300.

They traveled with a horse and wagon and sold a variety of medicines. These men were always talented entertainers, and they frequently used musicians or singers to make their performances even more exciting. These spectacles were called *medicine shows*. Many were like small carnivals.

The shows were often sponsored by a major patent-medicine manufacturer. Performers would often spend half a year on the road, traveling from one small town to another. If the show ran out of medicine, it was easy to get more. Supplies could be replenished at local drugstores or railway depots.

Medicine shows were a common sight in parts of the South as late as the 1920s. Today, the shows are part of the past. The few traces that remain include the brightly lithographed flyers, posters and trade cards passed out by the sellers. Many bottle collectors add these to their collections as *go-withs*. These are items that go with a particular patent-medicine bottle. They often bring more money than the bottles they promoted.

POPULARITY OF PATENT MEDICINES

Patent medicines were very popular because they had something to offer the buyer—hope. During the 19th century, medical treatment was often unavailable or inadequate. Patent medicines were the only remedy that many ill people could use.

Testimonials—Some people believed that the medicines actually cured them. One of the most effective ad-

vertising gimmicks employed by the sellers of patent medicines was the *testimonial*. This was a statement by someone who claimed to have been cured by the medicine. Such testimonials were usually placed on the bottle or in an advertisement. The following testimonial about bottled pills is typical:

"Since taking Tanlac I look and feel like a different person," recently asserted Mrs. Leslie Herbolzhiemer, 40 Portland Street, Worcester, Mass.

"Two years of stomach trouble brought on a complication of ills that were fast shattering my health. Indigestion kept me in constant pain and misery, and I actually did not have the strength to comb my hair. My nerves were so excited that I would wake up all hours of the night and loss of sleep was just wearing me out.

"As badly run down as I was, it has taken only six bottles of Tanlac to make me feel like my normal self. My troubles are not only gone, but I sleep like a child and have gained twenty pounds. My gratitude to Tanlac is unbounded."

Do you think Mrs. Herbolzhiemer was telling the truth? As you may have guessed, many of these testimonials were false. They were created to promote sales. Even so, there can be no doubt that some reflected sincere belief in a cure.

Contents of Patent Medicines—One reason for the popularity of patent medicines was that many contained alcohol or drugs. Consider Old Doctor Townsend's Sarsaparilla, a bottle popular with collectors. It was made with emerald-green glass and was often pontil-marked. The "medicine" in this bottle was actually sassafras bark, molasses and rye whiskey. Mrs. Winslow's Soothing Syrup was touted as a great pacifier for crying children. It probably was—one of its main ingredients was opium.

No one knows how many innocent people became alcoholics or drug addicts due to patent medicines. By the late 19th century, responsible doctors were taking a hard look at these concoctions. In 1905, *Collier's* magazine printed an article on proprietary medicines. The article revealed that most medicines contained alcohol. It claimed that 240 brands had such a high alcohol content that the sellers should have been licensed as saloons!

Some people had known for a long time that most patent medicines contained alcohol. The makers of non-alcoholic patent medicines had prospered by advertising that their competitors were selling whiskey. But the article in *Collier's* upset many more people. It led to the passage, in 1907, of the national Pure Food and Drug Act. It required disclosure of the contents of patent medicines.

This law and public disclosures of fraud led to a gradual decline in the sale and use of patent medicines. Other factors contributed to this decline. By 1900, doctors were receiving more modern, standardized training. They were beginning to understand the nature of many illnesses. As the treatment that doctors offered improved, there was less of a market for patent medicines. Even today, however, many remain on the market.

COLLECTING PATENT MEDICINES

There are so many patent-medicine bottles available that you may find it best to limit your efforts to one specific type of bottle. Bottles with pontil marks are a logical category, but they are somewhat difficult to find. One attractive category comprises *figural* bottles. These bottles are shaped like specific objects, such as animals or log cabins.

One example of a rare figural medicine bottle is a log-shaped one for Warner's Tippecanoe for Dyspepsia. Another is the odd, six-sided bottle used for Warner's Log Cabin Extract and for Warner's Log Cabin Cough and Consumption Remedy.

Some embossed figurals are very pretty. These include the green Pine Tree Jar Cordial bottle, with its distinctive pine tree. Another is the ever-popular bottle for Warner's Safe Kidney and Liver Cure. It has a safe embossed on the front.

Other Subcategories—Most collectors concentrate on buying bottles in a limited category of medicines. Some seek *specifics*—medicines designed to cure a single ailment. Some collectors want only *cures*, which offered remedies for many diseases.

In each case, the word is embossed on the bottle. Other sought-after categories are tonics, liniments, sarsaparillas, ointments, oils, pectorals, remedies, salves, restoratives, extracts, compounds, balsams and cordials. By focusing on bottles embossed with these or similar words, you can establish an enjoyable and interesting collection.

You might want to concentrate on medicines made by a single company. Many collectors are interested in

---

BUYING AND SELLING MEDICINE BOTTLES

- Always check the bottoms of medicine bottles for pontil marks. A pontil-marked bottle is always worth more than a similar, unmarked bottle.
- Look for bottles in unusual colors, such as deep blue, green, red and yellow. Most medicine bottles are in aqua, amber or clear glass. Colored examples are worth more.
- Medicine bottles are also more valuable in sets. For example, several different medicine bottles were used by the Warner Co. of Rochester, New York. If you collect a complete group of these, each bottle will be worth more than it would be if you owned only one.
- Watch for sample medicine bottles. These are much smaller than bottles in which the medicine was sold. Most sample bottles were given away to encourage people to try the medicine. They are relatively uncommon, and some bring high prices.
- Never remove the paper label from a medicine bottle. Most of these bottles have lost their labels, so the presence of one increases the value of the bottle. This is also true of the original contents.
- Medicine bottles usually command the highest prices in the areas where the bottles or contents were made. This is because many collectors concentrate on acquiring locally made products. For example, Dr. Kilmer remedies were manufactured in Binghamton, New York. This is where their bottles bring the highest prices.
- Most medicine bottles came in one size—about a pint-and-a-half capacity. However, some were made in two or three sizes. The smallest and largest are usually the rarest and most expensive. A bottle belonging to a set comprising all standard sizes for a particular medicine will be more valuable than a similar bottle that is not part of a set.
- Medicine bottles that were closed with a cork are older than those with screw caps. Usually they are more valuable, too.

---

bottles that held medicines manufactured by the H. H. Warner Co. of Rochester, New York. Warner bottles come in many varieties and several shapes. Acquiring all of them can be challenging.

Among the more interesting of these bottles are the ones made for sale in Canada. They include the address of Warner's distributors in Ontario and Quebec.

Whatever your choice, you will have little trouble finding medicine bottles. They are dug out of every bottle dump. Most antique shops have a few, and bottle shops and shows offer plenty. You will find that the prices for medicines are usually relatively low. Exceptions are bottles with pontil marks or unusual colors or decorations. Just remember to limit your collecting field. Otherwise, there will not be enough room in the house for both you and your collection!

Small medicine bottles are less common than larger ones. However, they are reasonably priced because they are not in great demand. Left: Hall's Catarrh Cure, from 1870 to 1900. Right: clear-glass Listerine bottle, from 1890 to 1910.

BITTERS BOTTLES

Bottles embossed or labeled with the word *bitters* are among the most collectible and valuable of all American bottles. More than 1,000 varieties of bitters bottles exist. These containers are especially interesting to collectors because of their various shapes, colors and embossings.

HISTORY OF BITTERS

The history of bitters is as interesting as the bottles. *Bitters* is a name for concoctions that comprise one type of patent medicine. Bitters usually consisted of a mixture of water, bitter herbs and a coloring agent. Most bitters also contained a lot of alcohol. In fact, it was the alcohol that first popularized bitters.

As early as the 17th century, European druggists and doctors were preparing folk medicines, which were called *bitters* because of their harsh taste. Bitters were quite popular in England. In the 18th century, England levied high taxes on gin. To avoid the tax, distillers mixed their liquor with herbs and called it *bitters*. This new concoction was an instant success in England. It was also popular in America, where rum was laced with herbs to avoid the crown's liquor tax.

Bottle Development—The first bitters bottles looked like ordinary medicine bottles. They had rectangular bodies, sloping shoulders and either open- or iron-pontil marks. Like medicine bottles, they were made from inexpensive aqua, green or amber glass.

No one knows when American bitters were put in embossed bottles for the first time. The early makers of bitters probably sold their products in labeled containers. By the 1840s, several manufacturers were selling and advertising bitters. These included Moses Atwood, John Moffat—producer of Phoenix Bitters—and S. O. Richardson.

By the middle of the 19th century, many brands of bitters were available. The manufacturers of most of these continued to use the traditional form of medicine bottle. However, many manufacturers began to produce figural containers. Some even experimented with more expensive colored glass or milk glass. Most people considered bitters as more than just another type of patent medicine. In many cases, they were a liquor.

The makers of whiskey flasks developed unusual and attractive shapes to catch the tippler's eye. Why shouldn't the makers of bitters do the same thing? The manufacturers of bitters turned to shape and color to help sell their product in an increasingly competitive market.

The figural bitters bottles are among the most desirable of all bottles. They include several different kinds of containers.

Kimball's Jaundice Bitters bottle from 1840 to 1850. Early pontil-marked bitters bottles, such as this one, are highly desirable.

John Moffat's Phoenix Bitters bottles come in more varieties than most bitters bottles. Colors range from aqua to amber. You'll find examples with and without pontil marks. Shown here are two rare types, both with pontil marks. Also shown is a tall Morning Bitters bottle with pontil mark.

SHAPES OF BITTERS BOTTLES

Some bitters bottles are barrel-shaped. The barrel shape was designed to remind the buyer of the whiskey barrel, from which much of the contents of bitters came. These bottles are found in many attractive colors, including blue, deep green, purple and yellow. Among the better-known brands are Greeley's, Pocahontas, Hall's, and Old Sachem.

Many bitters bottles were shaped like log cabins. This design played upon the theme of the frontiersman and his log cabin, popular during the 19th century. The bottles came in shades of amber and green. Brand names included Drake's Plantation Bitters, Kelly's Old Cabin and Lovegood's Family Bitters.

Many other figural types can be found. Berkshire Bitters came in a pig-shaped bottle. The Fish Bitters came in a fish-shaped bottle. Brown's Celebrated Indian Herb Bitters came in a container in the form of an Indian woman. An almost identical bottle was used by the manufacturers of Mohawk Pure Rye Whiskey. This was probably no coincidence—the two liquids contained about the same amount of alcohol.

Other interesting examples include National Bitters bottles, shaped like an ear of corn, and McKeever's Army Bitters bottles, which resembled a stack of cannonballs atop a drum. Simon's Centennial Bitters bottle was in the form of a bust of George Washington. Dingen's Napoleon Cocktail Bitters came in a clock-shaped bottle. The Panacea Bitters bottle was shaped like a lighthouse.

You can find other forms. Rare, attractive bottles are frequently expensive, costing as much as $1,000 per bottle.

Don't let the high prices of some bitters bottles discourage you. There are many inexpensive bitters containers, too. Among the less costly bottles are those produced in great quantities. Two good examples of inexpensive bitters bottles are Hostetter's and Atwood's.

Hostetter's bitters were estimated to be 94-proof. That means the bitters were more potent than most common whiskeys! Hostetter's was issued to Union troops during the Civil War as a prebattle "stimulant."

Much of the success of Hostetter's was the result of the manufacturer's understanding of advertising. Hostetter's was promoted through newspapers, on posters and in traveling medicine shows. The bottles were both embossed and labeled. Merchants selling Hostetter's were provided with elaborate tin signs to use as promotional devices.

Lash's was another popular and heavily advertised bitters. One of the trade cards issued by this company pictured the Wright brothers' biplane passing over lower Manhattan. The plane had a bottle of Lash's hanging from its fuselage! This trade card is a good example of the advertising stunts bitters manufacturers used at

The delicate curve of the neck of certain bottles has earned them the name *lady's leg*. This lady's-leg bitters bottle, marked Sazerac Aromatic Bitters, is made of white milk glass.

the end of the 19th century. The wonderful shapes of the bottles and the various advertising materials resulted from intense competition.

The most collectible bitters bottles are the figurals. Next are bottles with pontil marks, followed by containers that are both labeled and embossed. Last are bottles that are either embossed or have labels. Very few collectors seek bottles with labels only, so these containers are a good buy for the beginning collector.

Bitters bottles were made in enormous quantities. You can find them in most parts of the country. People find them in old barns and attics or dig for them. Many types are available in bottle and antique shops. Rarer types, such as figural and early pontiled bottles, are usually obtainable only from specialized dealers. You can also purchase them from other collectors or at auctions.

A Simon's Centennial Bitters bottle from the 1870s, in the form of a bust of George Washington. Figural bitters bottles are very popular.

Bitters bottles come in many different figural forms. Left to right: Harvey's Prairie Bitters, with pineapple-shaped top; a lady's-leg Canton Bitters bottle; and a tower-shaped Panacea Bitters bottle. All are rare.

BUYING AND SELLING BITTERS BOTTLES

• Be cautious when you buy *labeled bitters*. These are identified only by a paper label; the bottle is not embossed. Because the value of these bottles has increased so much in the past decade, unscrupulous people have made fake labels. Some have even cut out newspaper advertisements for bitters, put them on ordinary bottles, and tried to pass them as genuine labeled bitters.

• Many bitters bottles advertised in 19th-century newspapers have not yet been identified. Always be on the lookout for previously unrecorded bitters.

• Few bitters bottles were pontil-marked, so pontiled examples always bring premium prices.

• Condition has an enormous effect on the price of bitters bottles. A crack or a chip will reduce the value of a piece by as much as 50%. The more obvious the damage, the greater the decrease in value.

• Color also affects price. A bitters bottle in a rare color, such as blue or yellow, may bring thousands of dollars. A bitters bottle in a common color, such as aqua or amber, may bring only a few hundred dollars. Be familiar with the rare colors and watch for them!

• Also watch for advertising materials related to bitters. These include trade cards, posters, almanacs and premiums given away to promote the bitters. These items are valuable. A group of them, sold with the bitters bottle they advertise, will bring a good price.

• Bitters are in great demand. They can usually be sold most profitably at auction. Such sales attract large groups of eager buyers.

CANNING AND FOOD JARS

Canning jars, also known as fruit or preserve jars, are among the most popular and readily available of all American bottles. They have been produced in large quantities since the middle of the 19th century and are still being made. Many are extremely common and quite inexpensive; others are rare and costly. To be a wise collector, you must learn how to distinguish among them.

WAX SEALERS

The first American canning jars appeared in the 1820s. They belonged to a group of containers called *wax sealers*. Food to be preserved was placed in the bottle. Then the bottle was boiled to destroy harmful bacteria. After boiling was completed, hot wax was poured on top of the contents. A tin or cork lid covered the bottle. It could also be sealed by a piece of cloth wrapped around the top and tied in place.

Wax sealers are characterized by wide-flanged rims with inner ledges on which the top rests. Early examples are sometimes pontil-marked. The most common color is aqua, although some bottles, such as the rare Standard, are deep blue. The characteristic shape is round, with sloping shoulders and a short, thick neck. A few examples, such as the Potter & Bodine Air Tight Fruit Jar, are barrel-shaped.

MASON JARS

Although they were made for decades, wax sealers were never completely satisfactory. The wax, used to seal the jars, fractured easily. This resulted in leaks and spoiled food. This problem was solved in 1858, when John Landis Mason patented a screw-top jar with matching lid. This design, basically unchanged, remains in use today.

Many different companies made Mason jars, and you will find the name *Mason* embossed on jars in many different ways. In fact, there are so many Mason jars that some collectors specialize in this type alone.

The best-known type of Mason jar is one embossed *Mason's Patent Nov. 30th, 1858*. Many versions of this jar exist. You will find them embossed with the names of the firms—such as Whitney or Ball—that manufactured this type of jar. You may also find jars embossed with the initials of these firms or with decorations such as Maltese crosses and keystones.

A later Mason container, the Mason's Improved Jar, with a two-piece metal-and-glass lid, is also well-known.

The most desirable Mason jars are those made before the advent of bottle-making machines, early in the 20th century. These jars are characterized by tops that were ground smooth. Almost all were made with

Owl-shaped mustard jar with screw top, early 20th century. Certain foods, such as mustard, were often packed in figural bottles. The bottle shown here is one of the most popular of these containers.

Milk bottles from the early 20th century. Left to right: amber Big Elm Dairy Co.; half-pint clear-glass Hampden Creamery Co.; green quart-sized Altacrest Farms. The milk bottles shown here are interesting variations of the usual color and shape of such containers.

aqua or clear glass. You may, however, come across some examples made with amber glass and a few made with various shades of green glass.

OTHER CLOSURES

Although Mason jars were very popular, they were not the only canning jars. Manufacturers developed other jars that had ingenious closing devices. Some of these jars are worth looking for.

The most practical closing device was the bail closure, still in use. One of the first jars to have this device was the Canton Electric Fruit Jar. It is rare, not only because it has a bail closure, but also because of its deep-blue color.

Other manufacturers made jars with clamps and screws to secure the tops. Because most of these fastenings did not work well, the jars did not become popular and are now rare. These obscure canning jars are among the most desirable of all such bottles. They often bring very high prices.

If you decide to collect these rare canning jars, remember to pay special attention to the closure. Most collectors will not acquire a jar if the closure is not intact and functioning. An early bail-closure or clamp-type jar without the metal closure device is worth much less than a jar that still has it.

COLLECTING CANNING JARS

You can buy canning jars for reasonable prices at most bottle and antique shows. More recent examples are sometimes available in secondhand shops and flea markets. You may also find them in attics and barns. However, you'll seldom "find" rarer types. You'll have to buy them from other collectors or from specialized dealers.

FOOD CONTAINERS

The bottles in which commercial manufacturers packaged their food products are available in great numbers. Among the earliest and most interesting are containers used for pickles and condiments. Large bottles embossed with gothic arches and elaborate floral designs were used to store pickles. Bottles for Cathedral Pickles are sometimes pontil-marked. They were usually made with green or aqua glass. Smaller, narrow bottles with similar decorations are called *pepper sauces.* Both types are popular with collectors.

Mustard and ketchup containers came in many shapes and styles. Early mustard bottles were usually squat and square. Later examples include interesting forms such as a milk-glass owl with a screw top. Ketchup, too, came in figural bottles. One particular favorite is a clear-glass representation of Uncle Sam, produced by Flaccus Brothers.

Other foods also came in figural bottles. Don't be surprised if you find a vinegar bottle in the form of George Washington. You may also encounter a syrup container in carnival glass that looks like an ear of corn. There is also a maple-syrup container that looks like an old woman.

Most food bottles, however, have ordinary shapes. They are identified by embossing or by a paper label. The majority are made with clear, aqua or amber glass. A few are made in rarer colors, such as blue or green. For example, tall, 10-sided Huckleberry bottles are a deep-red amber.

COLLECTING FOOD BOTTLES

Food bottles are one of the best categories for the beginning collector. Most of the bottles are inexpensive, but there are exceptions. For example, early figural bottles and those that come in unusual colors are usually fairly expensive.

Vast numbers of food bottles were made after the introduction of automatic bottle-making machines. You can find these bottles everywhere. Homes, storehouses, old shops, secondhand stores and dumps are among the best places to look. These bottles are still unappreciated by most collectors, so you can assemble a satisfying collection at modest cost.

MILK BOTTLES

Milk bottles are closely related to food bottles. The first milk bottle was patented in 1880. Early milk bottles looked very much like those of today. They had low shoulders and a long, tapering neck. The first milk bottles were closed with a bail closure similar to that used on some canning jars.

By 1890, this closure had been replaced by what came to be the standard closure. It consisted of a shallow ledge inside the top of the bottle neck. The ledge held a disposable cardboard cap in place.

Almost all milk bottles are made of clear glass. The few colored types, such as the deep-green Altacrest Farms and the amber Big Elm Dairy bottles, are eagerly sought. The next-best thing to a colored milk bottle is an embossed milk bottle.

The embossing on milk bottles served an important function. Most bottles were intended for reuse. It was necessary to identify the bottle's source. Even so, some of the embossing on milk bottles is decorative. There are bottles featuring stars, American flags, buildings, cows, people milking cows and people carrying milk pails. You may also come across milk bottles with embossed birds. An eagle appears on many milk bottles, just as it does on many beer bottles. It can be fun trying to obtain as many varieties as possible.

Although relatively few collectors seek them, milk bottles are not always easy to find. Advertising in bottle-collecting publications is one good way to locate them.

Another is to scout out old dairies that have closed. You can also visit old grocery stores. Because milk bottles were generally returned for a deposit, very few are found in dumps or attics.

Although milk bottles can be hard to find, they are usually not expensive. Of course, you should expect to pay more for the colored bottles and for those with embossing.

CANDY CONTAINERS

Candy containers are among the most charming of all food containers. These small bottles are usually made with clear glass. You may find some pieces made with milk glass. Examples in colored glass, such as blue or yellow, are rare. On some pieces, the glass has been decorated with paint. Some candy containers also have cardboard or metal decorations.

Clear-glass candy container in the shape of a locomotive, early 20th century. Candy containers, most of which were made with clear glass, were popular from the early 1900s until the 1930s.

Clear-glass nursing bottle from the 1930s. Most nursing bottles were machine-made in the 20th century.

Large food-storage bottle from 1920 to 1930, embossed with the word *Planters* and large peanut shells. Large storage or serving bottles such as this were often used in grocery stores.

The earliest candy containers were a Liberty Bell and a representation of Philadelphia's Independence Hall. They were made during the 1876 centennial.

Most candy containers were made between 1900 and 1940. The majority were made with automatic bottle-making machines. During that period nearly 1,000 forms were created. They ranged from household objects, such as suitcases, clocks and radios, to vehicles, such as airplanes, automobiles and ships.

Numerous containers were made in the shapes of animals or people, including popular radio and comic-strip characters. All these containers were originally filled with tiny sugar candies. They were sold for a few cents in toy and candy stores and at tourist spots such as Niagara Falls.

Collecting candy containers is very popular, so early or rare examples are expensive. However, you will probably have little difficulty finding less expensive examples. Antique shows and shops are good places to look.

Unlike many bottles, candy containers are often carried by general antique dealers. These containers are frequently included with collections of toys or miniatures. The value of a candy container depends on how complete it is. If an item originally had a tin or pewter top, it will have less value if the top is missing. Always try to buy complete containers.

BUYING AND SELLING
CANNING AND FOOD BOTTLES

• The tops of most bottles are not important to collectors. However, canning jars came with a variety of metal closures. Without them the jars will be worth much less. Always try to buy jars and bottles with original tops. It's also a good idea to buy tops alone. You may later be able to match these with topless jars.

• Almost all canning jars were of aqua glass. Unusual colors, such as amber, yellow or green, bring high prices. You must be careful, however. Dishonest persons sometimes stain the interior of an ordinary jar amber or yellow. Scratch the jar just inside the neck or shoulder with a pin. If the color comes off, the jar has been stained.

• Most canning jars are inexpensive. They offer one of the best opportunities to acquire a large collection at relatively little cost. The many variations of the Mason jar are especially appealing to collectors.

• An enormous quantity of food bottles was produced during the past century. These bottles offer a promising field for the new collector. Look for unusual shapes. Even the contemporary Mrs. Butterworth's syrup bottle is collectible. Also watch for unusual colors and embossing.

• Because most food bottles were made with amber, aqua or clear glass, those made with green, blue or red glass are worth more. With the exception of early mustard, pickle and relish jars, few food containers were pontiled. A pontil mark, therefore, adds much to the bottle's value.

• Glass milk bottles are seldom seen today, so any 20th-century milk bottle is worth collecting. Examples with unusual colors, such as amber or green, are especially valuable. So are examples in odd sizes or with unusual closures or embossed decorations.

• Candy containers are most valuable when found complete with their original candy and with their tin or cardboard closures. Never discard the candy or closures. Likewise, never remove original paint or gilding. These also enhance the value of a piece.

Flaccus Brothers Steers Head Fruit Jar in green glass. These jars are difficult to find. Notice their unusual glass screw closures.

Canning jars with iron-pontil marks, 1850 to 1860. Left: airtight fruit jar. Right: Potter & Bodine's airtight fruit jar, Philadelphia. Early canning jars were referred to as *wax sealers* and often had tin lids. They are rare and valuable.

Canning or fruit jars in blue are particularly rare and desirable. Left to right: wax sealer without embossing; wax sealer embossed with *W;* Canton Electric Fruit Jar with bail closure; wax sealer embossed with *Standard.* The Canton Electric Fruit Jar is one of the most prized of all canning jars.

Few figural bottles are made today. Collectors prize those that are produced. This amber Mrs. Butterworth's syrup bottle is still being made. It will certainly increase in value.

Milk bottles are wonderful collectibles. This clear-glass example was made between 1920 and 1940. The ribbed body is appealing. In those days, milk cost a nickel per quart.

MINERAL-WATER AND SODA-WATER BOTTLES

Some mineral waters, and all soda waters, are bubbly. The bubbles in most mineral waters are the result of natural ingredients, usually mineral salts found in springs. The bubbles in soda water are the result of impregnating the water with carbonic gas. Bottles that contained these sparkling waters are very popular with collectors. Both kinds are easy to find, and both make interesting collections.

MINERAL-WATER BOTTLES

Mineral waters are usually bottled under pressure to maintain their bubbles, or *effervescence*. Because of the pressure, a strong bottle is required. A typical mineral-water bottle is heavy and squat with high, sloping shoulders.

Most mineral-water bottles have lips with double rims. The lips consist of a narrow rim that has a broader rim on top of it. The most common color for mineral-water bottles is dark green. You may also find a few aqua and amber examples. Yellow, pale green or red-amber bottles are harder to find. The great majority of mineral-water bottles have the smooth bottom associated with the snap-case method.

Few early mineral-water bottles with open-pontil marks can be found. Examples with iron-pontil marks are less scarce. Early examples bring higher prices than bottles made later.

Some mineral-water bottles have a *kick-up*—a raised, hollow area at the bottom of the bottle. You find the same kick-up on champagne bottles. Both champagne and mineral waters are bottled under pressure. The kick-up strengthens the bottom of the bottle.

Some History—Mineral waters don't always have a pleasant taste. The purpose of these waters has always been medicinal. And medicine isn't always tasty.

Mineral waters have a long history. As early as A.D. 77, the famous historian Pliny made a list of Europe's important mineral springs. Early settlers in North America found Indians bathing in and drinking mineral waters. The so-called High Rock Spring at Saratoga, New York, was visited by settlers in 1761. Six years later, waters from Jackson's Spa in Boston were being bottled and sold.

It was not until the 1820s that special bottles were designed for mineral water. The first were manufactured for Lynch & Clark of New York City, a well-known distributor of mineral waters. These bottles were pontiled and were of the typical design. They are now quite rare.

Seltzer bottles, such as the one above, were common in New York and other cities, but have now become expensive. The top of the bottle contains a mechanism for dispensing the seltzer.

Mineral-water bottles have thick sides and a squat form, characteristics necessary to assure that they could contain effervescent liquids stored within them. Shown here are a pint Congress and Empire Springs, a quart Missisquoi Springs with embossed figure of an Indian, and a quart Knowlton Saratoga.

Mineral baths and mineral waters were found at *spas*. The heyday of spas was from 1850 to 1890. Most mineral-water bottles date from that period.

Mineral-water bottles are usually embossed with the name of a particular spring or the name of a distributor. You can collect bottles from across the country, or you can concentrate on a single area or even a single spa.

Favorite Mineral-Bottle Types—Saratoga Springs, New York, is a favorite with collectors. Several dozen springs have been established there. Some are *artesian,* or free-flowing, but most were dug. Many of these springs have been given interesting names, such as Congress, Saratoga A, Hathorn and Washington. Many bottles have one of these names embossed on them. It is possible to acquire a substantial collection of marked Saratoga mineral-water bottles.

You can find marked examples from other areas, too. Towns such as Ballston and Round Lake in New York state, Sheldon in Vermont and various Massachusetts communities have been memorialized on mineral-water bottles. The most eagerly sought mineral-water bottles are the few that have both embossed pictures and words. The bottles used for the waters from Washington Springs at Ballston have a bust of George Washington. The containers from Saratoga's High Rock Spring are adorned with a crude representation of a rock.

Figural mineral-water bottles are very rare. Indeed, only a single type exists—that of the Poland Springs at Poland, Maine. This bottle is in the form of an old man with a long beard sitting on a rock. It is popularly known as the *Moses bottle*. The form alludes to the biblical tale of Moses striking his staff on a rock and causing water to flow forth. These bottles usually come in light amber or clear glass. More than 40 variations of the Moses bottle have been produced. Not all of these have been used for mineral water.

Collecting Mineral-Water Bottles—Great collector interest in the past few years has driven up the prices of mineral-water bottles. A rare example can now cost several hundred dollars. However, most remain inexpensive. Because the bottles were made in large quantities and are so durable, they are easy to find. You should have no trouble locating them at shows or in shops. Dumps and cellars are other good places to look.

SODA-WATER BOTTLES

Most soda-water bottles are smaller than mineral-water bottles. They are also shaped differently. Mineral-water bottles are usually quart size, although pints are also found. Soda-water bottles are typically a pint or smaller.

Soda-water bottles were designed to hold plain carbonated water—water saturated with carbonic gas. The gas was the source of the bubble. This created pressure similar to the pressure of gaseous mineral water. Therefore, soda-water bottles, like mineral-water bottles, were made strong. Most early soda-water bottles are of thick glass with low, sloping shoulders, a long neck and a large *blob top*. In some cases, the bottom has a shallow kick-up.

An interesting soda-water bottle that you may encounter is the *torpedo*. Its name is derived from its shape. It has a bottom so narrow and rounded that many examples cannot be made to stand. The design was deliberate. Bottles were stoppered with corks, which could dry out if the bottle was upright for a long time. This ruined the contents due to gas escaping through the cracked cork. A bottle stored on its side would keep the cork moist and avoid the problem.

Some History—The first soda-water bottles appeared in the 1830s. It was at this time that John Matthews of New York City, one of the first mass producers, made 25 million gallons of soda water. Matthews' soda is memorable because its bubbles were created from ground-up marble chips left over from the building of Saint Patrick's Cathedral! The chips were broken down to form carbonic acid.

Early soda-water bottles were pontiled. Most carried the iron-pontil mark. From 1879, *Hutchinson devices,* which worked like plungers, were used to seal soda bottles. In 1891, the crown cap was developed. It is still in use.

The glass of early soda-water bottles came in aqua, green or sometimes a rich blue. The latter is one of the most desirable colors for collectors. The embossing on these early bottles usually included only the name and address of the distributor.

During the late 1800s, soda-water bottles began changing. Larger bottles were introduced for use in shipment and bulk storage. Most of these were made with clear glass. The embossing on these bottles was sometimes very elaborate. One well-known quart soda bottle bore a representation of a clerk pouring out a glass of soda water.

By the late 19th century, flavored sodas caught on with the public. By 1900, several *soda pops,* as they were called, were for sale. They included Coca-Cola, Pepsi Cola, root beer and Moxie. Bottles for these were made in great numbers and varieties.

Collecting Soda-Water Bottles—Soda-bottle collectors vary in their interests. Some collect the earliest pontiled bottles. Others look for the unusual torpedo or for bottles with 8- or 12-sided shapes. Some seek unusual colors, such as blue or deep green. You may find it most interesting to concentrate on embossing—especially the marks of a particular area or community.

Collectors of soda-pop bottles usually try to get all the available variations of a particular type or color. Coca-Cola bottles in particular are found in great varieties. Each bottling plant had bottles embossed with its location. You may wish to limit your collection to your state or even your city. The types, colors and forms available can satisfy a wide range of collecting tastes.

Except for the oldest and rarest forms, sodas are readily available. You can find them at most bottle shows and in most shops. You can also find good examples in old dumps or forgotten storage places.

BUYING AND SELLING MINERAL-WATER AND SODA BOTTLES

- Most mineral-water bottles have similar shapes and were made with green or black glass. One factor that increases the value of a mineral-water bottle is the embossed name of the mineral spring. Two other features that increase the value are pontil marks and unusual colors.
- Dumps and old wells are good places to look for mineral-water bottles. Because these bottles are so durable, many are found intact.
- The value of soda bottles is enhanced by unusual shapes. Look for bottles that have 6, 8 or 12 sides. Also watch for bottles with a *lightning stopper*. It consists of a metal or porcelain lid, held with a wire fastener. Soda bottles that still have this device are worth more than those that do not. Soda bottles prized most by collectors are pontiled examples made of blue glass.
- Bottles of later sodas, such as Coca-Cola, Pepsi and Moxie, are easy to find. The highest prices are paid for rare forms, particularly those discontinued after being used only a short time. Unusual colors, such as orange carnival glass, also bring premium prices.
- An interesting and inexpensive collection can be made with Coca-Cola bottles bearing the embossed names of the towns in which bottling firms were located. There are hundreds of these companies. A bottle that is part of such a collection is worth more than a similar bottle that is not.

FLASKS

There are many different kinds of whiskey bottles. The most popular—and the aristocrats of the whiskeys—are the small, flattened, egg-shaped bottles known as *flasks*.

EARLIEST FLASKS

Flasks have been made in America for many years. They were advertised as early as the 1750s. Most flasks were used to sell small amounts of whiskey. They had only a half-pint or pint capacity. Their flattened form made them easier to slip into a pocket.

The earliest flasks were quite different from those people collect now. During the 1790s, a Maryland factory made clear-glass receptacles engraved with names, dates and decorative designs. Their shapes resembled later flasks, but the sophisticated engraving was done by hand.

Pitkin flasks appeared during the late 18th and early 19th centuries. These distinctive containers were made at the Pitkin Glass Works of East Hartford, Connecticut, and at several shops in the Midwest. These vessels had the flattened shape of later flasks, but longer necks. They were dark green or aqua and were shaped in a dip mold. Although these bottles are attractive collectors' items, few makers can be identified. These vessels do not bear names or decorations, and similar bottles were made in Europe at the same time.

FIGURAL FLASKS

About 1810, a type of flask appeared that was shaped similar to its predecessors, but bore very different decorations. Collectors call these bottles *figural flasks*. These containers were blown in molds carved in a variety of shapes with intricate surface decorations. They appeared about the same time as American embossed medicine bottles. They were mainly designed for effective advertising.

Flasks were designed to promote the sale of whiskey, rum and gin in relatively small, prepackaged amounts. Before the development of flasks, such beverages had been sold primarily from barrels in stores and taverns. Customers either supplied their own container or drank their purchase on the spot. Liquor sold this way was extremely inexpensive—as little as 3 cents a pint—so the profit margin was small. To promote sales and justify higher prices, distillers developed colorful flasks for their wares.

Figural flasks were an immediate hit. During the period of their greatest popularity, about 1820 to 1890, more than 700 types appeared. As is the case with modern Jim Beam bottles, these flasks were collected as soon as they were available for sale.

Violin, or scroll, flasks from 1830 to 1850. Scroll flasks are usually pontil-marked. Rare colors bring high prices.

Very few figural flasks are found in dumps because they were rarely discarded. By 1900, substantial collections had been formed. Today, an army of collectors pursues figural flasks. Prices, other than those for rarities, are standardized. Even the most common flasks, such as cornucopia and urn designs, sell for at least $50. Harder-to-find examples run into the hundreds and even thousands of dollars. As much as $25,000 has been paid for one flask!

FLASK CATEGORIES

Collectors recognize two broad categories of flasks: historical and pictorial.

Historical Flasks—Historical pieces are those on which the embossed decoration consists of presidential portraits, national or international figures, or patriotic symbols. Nearly 60 flasks bear the bust of George Washington. The likenesses of John Quincy Adams, Andrew Jackson, William Henry Harrison, Zachary Taylor and William McKinley are also popular.

Other famous individuals also appear on flasks. You may recognize Lafayette, Henry Clay, William Jennings Bryan and the 19th-century Hungarian writer and patriot Louis (Lajos) Kossuth. You will even see Jenny Lind, the famous Swedish singer who toured America under the auspices of the great showman P. T. Barnum.

Patriotic symbols include representations of Uncle Sam, the American eagle, and various stars and flags. Some collectors include in this category flasks embossed with objects such as a cornucopia or a sheaf of wheat. Other symbols that may be considered either patriotic or pictorial include cornstalks, trains or an urn overflowing with fruit. All these were meant to represent the growth and prosperity of America.

Pictorial Flasks—The second, and larger, category of flasks is pictorial. These are flasks with embossing that is purely decorative. The embossing may include sporting scenes, such as the hunter and the fisherman on the Hunter-Fisherman calabash-shaped bottle. Humorous figures are featured, too, such as the hobolike gold prospector on the Pikes Peak flask. Another humorous flask shows a girl riding an old "bone-crusher" bicycle. This scene adorns the Not For Joe flask.

Pictorial flasks include representations of log cabins, trees and even a glassworks. Animals were not forgotten either. Dogs, deer and ducks appear on flasks. Especially popular with collectors are the flasks bearing embossed representations of racehorses. The best known is the Flora Temple calabash-shaped bottle, which memorializes a 19th-century trotter.

MASONIC FLASKS

The Masons were an extremely powerful organization during the early 19th century. Many important national figures, including Andrew Jackson, were members. Nearly 40 flasks bear symbols of the Masonic

Pontil-marked sunburst flasks from 1815 to 1835. Named for the embossed rays covering their sides, sunburst flasks are among the earliest American flasks. Examples in clear glass are rare.

Pair of clear-glass flasks commemorating the 1896 presidential election. One flask is embossed *In McKinley We Trust;* the other, *In Bryan We Trust.* William McKinley won the election and became the nation's 25th president.

Flasks with Masonic symbols and pontil marks, 1815 to 1830. Left to right: Masonic symbols and eagle over the embossed word *Keene;* Masonic symbols with Lafayette on reverse side; Masonic symbols with eagle on reverse side. During the late 19th century, the Masons were politically powerful in the United States.

Calabash bottle from 1845 to 1855. The bottle is embossed with a sheaf of wheat and a star. It has an iron-pontil mark and an unusual handle.

society, forming an interesting subcategory. Some of these flasks can be classified as pictorial; others as historical.

Most Masonic flasks date from 1815 to 1830. The organization lost much of its following during the 1830s.

OTHER FLASKS

Approximately 400 flask types were made before 1850. Pontil marks are more common on them than on any other category. These flasks are wonderful collectibles. You can divide them into several categories.

Sunburst Flasks—Several important groups of flasks are distinguished more by their form than by their decoration. The most prominent are the *sunburst flasks.* These vessels have square shoulders and ridged sides. They get their name from the characteristic embossed rays extending from a central point on each side. The sunburst motif is also found on late 18th- and early 19th-century furniture in the Federal style.

Sunburst flasks are a wonderful reflection of an important period in American design. The earliest known American flask, from the Pitkin factory about 1810, features a sunburst.

Although 30 variations are known, sunburst flasks are hard to find and command high prices.

Scroll Flasks—The *scroll,* or *violin,* flask is much easier to find. This pear-shaped bottle comes in several sizes, ranging from the common half-pint to the rare gallon size. They come in many colors—aqua, amber, dark green, blue, pale green, yellow, red, amethyst, gray, violet, purple and moonstone. You could easily assemble an imposing collection by concentrating on this category alone.

Rare colors and sizes can be expensive. However, you may find one of the more common flasks, such as the aqua scroll flask, for $50 to $60.

A rarer type of flask is the concentric ring eagle. This vessel is completely round—except for the neck—and has an eagle embossed on each side. Its circular form is unique among American flasks. The flask body is covered with heavy embossed ridges or *rings.*

Calabashes—This is another unusual form of flask. The tall, usually quart-capacity, vessel has a long neck and a body that is more round than flattened—similar to a calabash gourd. Calabashes appear to have been copied from whiskey bottles of similar shape. A few examples even have handles, like those on some whiskey bottles.

Calabashes were apparently never very popular. They were made for less than a decade during the 1850s. They were made in considerable quantities, however, and several kinds are easy to find. You should have no difficulty locating one of the Jenny Lind calabashes, for example.

Political Flasks—Flasks with political representations are also interesting. All political flasks have two sides, and the majority have a different design on each. In most cases, this was done to liven up the piece and make it more appealing to purchasers. In some cases, however, it reflected a secondary, political purpose.

Many flasks were advertisements for political candidates. For example, a series of Washington-Taylor flasks, in gorgeous colors, was manufactured when Zachary Taylor was running for president. The flasks were passed out in the streets or at political rallies. When the drinker raised the flask to his lips, he was looking at the embossed busts of two great patriots—George Washington and Zachary Taylor. Did the idea work? Well, Taylor became the 12th president of the United States.

Flasks were so effective for this purpose during the 19th century because drinking near polling places was permitted. Stores selling liquor were not closed during voting hours. Giving a man—women could not vote—a drink to encourage him to vote for a specific candidate was perfectly normal and legal.

LATER FLASKS

During the 19th century, the form and quality of flasks gradually changed. Those made before 1850 tend to be either highly stylized representations of objects or portraits of people. In either case, they were made from well-carved molds and often were produced in several colors. After 1850, the quality declined. Although the variety increased, the pictorial elements were not well done. Plain, unembossed flasks also began to appear.

The earliest of the simpler vessels were marked *Traveler's Companion*. They came in green or amber glass and were often embossed with a simple star or teardrop.

By the 1870s, almost all *hip flasks,* as they were then called, were embossed with nothing more than the name of a particular brand of whiskey and capacity. Many were not embossed at all. They were made with aqua or clear glass only.

You should bear in mind that clear glass was neither easier nor less expensive to make than colored glass. In fact, clear glass had been extremely rare in early flasks because of the difficulty of removing iron impurities. These impurities gave glass an aquamarine or amber tint. Clear glass became most popular when new processes made it less time-consuming and costly to purify the glass.

Most of these later flasks are of little interest to collectors of figural flasks. They can usually be found in large quantities and cost very little. Although they may not seem as interesting as earlier examples, they are part of a tradition that continues today in pint-size, machine-made hip flasks.

Some of these later flasks do bear the embossed name of a glassworks. In general, figural flasks are more likely to bear a glassmaker's mark than other vessels. The reasons for this are not clear. The glassmakers were probably proud of their work and wanted the world to

Traveler's Companion flasks. Left: green flask, marked *Lockport Glass Works.* Dates from 1840 to 1850. Right: amber flask, marked *Ravenna Glass Co.* Dates from 1850 to 1870. Relatively few flasks—or other bottles—bear the marks of the glassworks where they were made.

Many clear-glass whiskey flasks were made during the late 19th century. These two were made between 1880 and 1910.

know that they had done it. Some of the more popular designs were widely copied, and a company mark tended to discourage this.

COLLECTING FLASKS

In light of the value and popularity of figural flasks, it is not surprising that more modern reproductions have been made. During the 1930s, a firm in Czechoslovakia turned out an excellent reproduction of the Jenny Lind calabash. This piece is now regarded as a collectible in its own right.

Clevenger Bros. of New Jersey has manufactured reproductions of various flasks. Some were made as souvenirs for glass-collectors' conventions and are so marked. Others are not so easily recognizable.

Clevenger Bros. has made several reproductions of the scroll flask. These closely resemble the originals except for the colors, which may differ from 19th-century examples.

Clevenger bottles are usually impressed on the base with a small *c*. Unfortunately, this letter can be ground off. Because pontil-marked Clevenger flasks are well made, the novice collector may have difficulty distinguishing them from the originals.

Flasks have been free-blown in both Europe and Mexico. In both cases, the forms differ from those of 19th-century examples and the colors are bright and unnatural. If you have studied authentic American flasks, you will not be fooled by these reproductions.

Many flasklike bottles are now on the market. Most are new creations rather than reproductions. The Lestoil bottles of the 1970s are the best known. Some of these have already become collectors' items.

As with any valuable item, you should always get a guarantee of authenticity from the seller when buying an expensive flask or bottle.

You can buy flasks from bottle dealers, at auctions or from other collectors. Very few general antique stores stock flasks. When they do, they usually handle only the more ordinary examples.

Broken Flasks—Because of their inherent value, broken flasks are often repaired. Because restored flasks are quite common, you should watch out for them. Chipped lips can be ground down. Broken pieces can be glued on. Even missing pieces can be replaced through the use of various epoxies and resins. Many collectors employ ultraviolet radiation, or *black light,* to examine flasks. Always examine prospective purchases very carefully. You should never pay as much for a repaired flask as you would for an undamaged one.

BUYING AND SELLING FLASKS

- Flasks have been collected for many years, so the prices for most types are relatively stable. You should never buy or sell a flask without first consulting a standard price guide. Because so many flasks were pontil-marked, the presence of such a mark does not greatly increase the value.
- Rarity of form and color are important factors in determining flask value. An aqua scroll flask may be worth $50 to $75. The same flask in a rare shade, such as blue or red, could bring more than $1,000. Before you buy or sell a flask, find out whether its color is rare.
- Flasks that are reproductions, and modern flask types—such as the Lestoil bottles—have relatively less value. If you have any doubts about the authenticity of a flask, consult an expert. Never purchase an expensive flask without getting a written guarantee of authenticity from the seller.
- Identical flask forms were often made with glass of different colors. You may want to collect a specific type of flask, such as a Washington-Taylor, in several hues. Each bottle in such a collection would be more valuable than it would be individually.
- Because they have been collected for so long, a specific flask may often have been in several collections. A flask has a higher value if it has been owned by an important collector. Many collectors put their names or other identifying marks on the bottoms of flasks they owned. Such marks should never be removed. Charles Gardner and George McKearin are two important collectors to look for.
- Flasks sold at auction usually bring the highest prices. It is best to use auction houses specializing in glass sales. Two such houses are Garth's in Ohio and Skinner's in Massachusetts. A major bottle auction will bring out the most eager and prosperous collectors. Flasks should never be sold as a small lot in a large, general auction. Containers sold this way may bring only a fraction of their real value.
- If you find a flask that is not in one of the major books on bottles, do not assume it is a fake or reproduction. It could be a rare, unrecorded example. Many flasks that were advertised in the 19th century have not yet been found or recognized. You might find one!
- Don't buy damaged flasks. Most serious collectors will not purchase them unless they are an extremely rare type. If you do buy a cracked or chipped flask, you will probably be unable to sell it—even at a bargain price.

BEER, WINE AND WHISKEY BOTTLES

Beers, wines and whiskeys have been consumed around the world in large quantities for centuries. The variety among these beverages is enormous. So is the selection of bottles and containers.

BEER BOTTLES

Collecting beer bottles is a relatively new hobby. It is an especially exciting area of bottle collecting. Many interesting examples are easy to find, and prices are still reasonably low.

Beer has long been a popular American drink, but it has not always been sold in bottles. Until the middle of the 19th century, the foaming brew was sold from large barrels. If you wanted to buy it, you had to take your own bottle to the store or brewery. Most Americans used bottles made of heavy black glass or of stoneware when purchasing beer. These bottles were shaped like mineral-water bottles. Those made of glass rarely bore identifying markings.

First Beer Bottles—The first bottles made especially for beer appeared about 1850. They were squat and heavy, had long necks and thick, doughnutlike blob tops. They came in pint and half-pint sizes and resembled the soda-water bottles of the same period. Beer bottles came in shades of green or aqua. The earliest examples were marked with an iron pontil.

You won't have much trouble identifying early beer bottles. Most of them carried embossed words, usually *porter* or *ale*. The word *beer* didn't appear on bottles until the 1870s. By then, the shape of the bottles had changed. They were taller and thinner and were usually made of aqua, clear or amber glass. Eventually, amber became the preferred color. Manufacturers believed that the dark glass protected the beer from the harmful effects of ultraviolet radiation, which destroys carbonation.

As with most bottles, early beer bottles were stoppered with corks. In 1879, the Hutchinson device was invented, and it soon replaced corks. You may come upon bottles that originally had Hutchinson stoppers, but have lost them. These are easy to spot because there is usually a piece of wire around the neck of the bottle. This wire represents the last remnant of the stopper. These bottles are not as valuable as those with complete stoppers.

Bottles from the late 19th century and the early 20th century are frequently unearthed by bottle diggers. You should have little difficulty finding good examples at reasonable prices. However, early pontil-marked porter and ale bottles are difficult to find today. So are bottles made in odd colors, such as blue and yellow.

Embossed Decorations—By the turn of the century, most beer bottles were embossed with the name of the

Early beer bottles were short, squat and usually made with green glass.

Beer bottles from 1880 to 1910. Left to right: amber Rochester, N.Y., Brewing Co.; Washington Brewing Co.; The George Bechtel Brewing Co.

Most early wine and spirits bottles used in America were made abroad in the 17th and 18th centuries and imported. All are pontil-marked. They are popular with American collectors.

Wine bottles, 1870 to 1920. Made with various shades of green and amber glass, these common, unembossed bottles are especially attractive when displayed against a light.

Pontiled case-gin bottle, 1820 to 1850. Gin bottles have been made in large quantities for two centuries. Late 19th-century examples sell for as little as $10 each. Earlier and larger pontiled gin bottles can be worth several hundred dollars each.

brewery. Many beer bottles were also made with elaborate embossed decorations. This wonderful array of embossed designs provides one of the great incentives for collecting beer bottles. The decorations range from a bust of George Washington above an eagle to an armed man carrying a flag.

Beer Breweries—You may find it particularly rewarding to collect bottles made by breweries in your hometown or some other specific locality. Local interest has always played a big part in beer-bottle collecting.

Today, there are fewer than 50 brewing companies in the United States. Not long ago, there were more than 50 in some large cities! For example, in 1879, Philadelphia had 94 breweries. Today it has only two.

You can research the breweries in your town by referring to old city directories in a library. You can also consult old newspapers or the archives at the chamber of commerce. A complete collection of beer bottles from each brewery in a city or community would be worth far more than the total value of all the individual bottles.

Beer Cans—Beer cans, which first appeared in 1935, have largely replaced bottles. Therefore, almost any beer bottle you find, even if it was made yesterday, will someday become a sought-after collectible.

WINE AND SPIRITS BOTTLES

Whiskey bottles constitute a diverse group. They provide opportunities for collectors of all ages, financial means and interests. In addition to medicine bottles, whiskey bottles offer the best way to acquire a large and varied collection quickly and inexpensively.

The enormous number of wine and spirits bottles available reflects the importance of alcohol in the history of America. The strict laws governing the manufacture of wine and hard liquor are relatively recent. Before the Civil War, people in most states could make and sell wine and liquor as they saw fit.

Early Wine and Liquor Bottles—Until well into the 19th century, most workingmen regarded whiskey or hard cider on the job as a necessity. They carried small flasks filled with hard liquor into fields and shops. Barn-raisings and other public construction efforts were regarded as incomplete without a barrel of cider. Sailors at sea expected a daily ration of rum.

Not everyone agreed with this custom, and there were prohibition movements throughout the 19th century. The drinking worker was not always the most efficient worker. Alcohol and job safety were certainly not compatible. Men fell off buildings they were roofing or were struck by trees they were felling. However, it was not until the prohibition movement gained momentum, early in the 20th century, that serious legal restraints were placed on alcoholic beverages.

Because of the popularity of wine and spirits, a

Several 19th-century whiskey bottles are shaped like cannons—perhaps a reminder of the bottles' powerful contents. These examples were made between 1870 and 1880. Left: J. T. Gayon, Alton. Right: Buchanan's Extract of Sugar Corn.

Political whiskey flask, embossed *Our Choice, Cleve & Steve* and dated *November 8th 92* and *March 4th 93*. This bottle was a souvenir of Grover Cleveland's successful 1892 presidential campaign.

large quantity of 18th-century and early-19th-century wine and liquor bottles remain. The earliest of these bottles were made with dark or aqua glass. They had squat, bulbous bodies, long necks ending in crude, banded rims, and high kick-up bottoms. Free-blown, with rough, open-pontil marks, many of these bottles look as though they had been shaped from bubble gum.

Most of these early liquor bottles were made in England or Holland and imported. Experts can discern differences in the ways they were made in each country. The bottles usually lack any marks that make easy determination of origins possible.

American-Made Bottles—Black-glass spirits bottles were made in America at a very early date. For example, the Germantown Glass Works near Braintree, Massachusetts, was producing them in the 1680s. They were probably made at every American glassworks about that time.

By the end of the 18th century, the shape of wine and whiskey bottles had begun to change. Some types, often called *chestnut* or *Ludlow* bottles, remained essentially squat and bulbous, but were flattened front and back. These bottles resembled chestnuts. They come in a range of sizes, from half-pint bottles to 20-gallon storage containers called *carboys.*

IDENTIFYING WINE AND WHISKEY BOTTLES

You will have little difficulty distinguishing between wine and whiskey bottles. By 1820 the differences between the two were well-established. Wine bottles had long, gently sloping shoulders and sometimes a kick-up base similar to those on early spirits bottles. Whiskey bottles had high, square shoulders and a heavy, rounded rim.

Until the 1850s, both kinds of bottles were sometimes pontil-marked and were usually made with amber glass. You may find some wine bottles in pretty hues, such as teal, sea green and dark red. Pay special attention to these bottles—they are highly prized by collectors.

Wine Bottles—The standard wine bottle, familiar to you, appeared about the end of the 18th century. It has changed little since then. It is cylindrical, with straight sides and a shorter neck than most other bottles.

Gin Bottles—Gin was invented in the 17th century and a new kind of bottle—the *case bottle*—was developed for it. The bottle was designed to fit into wooden packing cases. The gin bottle had a square base and sides that tapered into broad shoulders. Above the shoulders was a relatively narrow neck and a collared or disklike rim. The bottle was usually made of dark-green glass.

Small amber whiskey sampler, or taster, in the form of a pistol, with a tin screw top. Dates from the late 19th century or the early 20th century. Pieces of this sort were sold for a few cents, or even given away, to promote a saloon or whiskey brand.

Whiskey sampler or cologne bottle in black milk-glass with a pewter top. It was made in the late 19th century. The shoe with protruding toe—a typical tramp motif—is usually associated with whiskey.

Seal Bottles—You should pay particular attention to *seal bottles,* first produced in Europe in the 17th century. These bottles bear a lump of glass—like a blob of sealing wax—imprinted with the name or initials of an owner or a manufacturer. Sometimes the seal includes a date.

Seal bottles, which were usually made to order, are rare and expensive. These vessels often had value as soon as they were made. In the 19th century, stores sometimes charged a deposit to ensure the return of seal bottles. This is still done in parts of Europe.

Owners who could not afford seal bottles sometimes painted their names on bottles.

Embossed Whiskey Bottles—By the 1820s, many spirits bottles, even the plainest, were made in two-piece molds. The use of molds provided the opportunity for advertising on these bottles, just as it had on medicine and bitters bottles.

By the 1830s, embossed whiskey bottles had appeared. Among the best-known is the red-amber Chestnut Grove whiskey bottle by C. W. Wharton. Others include the C. E. Burrows and Bininger bottles from New York City.

You are likely to come across some cylindrical whiskey bottles. However, most whiskey bottles were made in the square, straight-sided design also used for medicine bottles. This resemblance indicated the blurred distinction between alcohol and patent medicine. Whiskey bottles were also designed this way because embossed advertising could be applied more effectively on flat surfaces.

Pay particular attention to the early embossed whiskey bottles made for A. M. Bininger and Co. of New York City. Bininger was a grocery and dry goods firm that had a line of bottles made for its alcoholic beverages. Among the earlier square whiskey bottles used by this firm are those marked *Bininger's Golden Apple Cordial* and *Bininger's Old Dominion Wheat Tonic. Tonic* was just another word for whiskey!

A similar container, popular with collectors, is marked *Monk's Old Bourbon/Whiskey/For Medicinal Purposes.* The use of phrases such as *for medicinal purposes* reflects the growing influence of prohibitionists on liquor advertising.

Figural whiskey samplers in the form of a pig, 1870 to 1890. Left to right: Berkshire Bitters; Duffy's Crescent Saloon; Good Old Bourbon In a Hog's—. These novelty items are very popular with collectors and bring high prices.

Milk-glass figural bottles. Left: Sitting bear. The bear bottle was typically filled with Kummel, a strong European liquor. Right: Atterbury Duck.

COLLECTING WHISKEY BOTTLES

Square and cylindrical whiskey bottles are still being made, and they are still being embossed. You should note the color of the glass. Until the 1870s, almost all whiskey bottles were made with amber glass. By 1900, bottles made with clear glass were common.

Clear-glass embossed bottles are among the most common and least expensive whiskey bottles. You can find them at old dumps and in storage places. You can also obtain them at antique stores and from bottle dealers—usually at very reasonable prices.

You will find that most collectors concentrate on

The Jolly Golfer liquor bottle in frosted blue glass, late 19th century. Like many figural bottles, this one could have been made in either Europe or the United States.

one type of whiskey bottle. Some concentrate on a specific distiller or distributor, or on bottles from a particular city or locality. Even if you choose to limit your collection in this way, you will find an ample selection of bottles.

FIGURAL WHISKEY BOTTLES

Figural whiskey bottles are the most desirable collectible whiskey containers. They are also among the most expensive. They resemble figural bitters bottles. This is not a coincidence. Both types of bottles were designed with the same goal in mind—to attract customers.

The earliest figural whiskey bottles had classical forms. Some were bell-shaped. Others had the graceful rounded shoulders and flaring lip of a Greek vase. Some closely resembled figural flasks, although the whiskey bottles had longer necks. Most had a common characteristic—an ear-shaped handle that was attached after the bottle had been removed from the mold. These bottles, also known as *handled whiskey jugs*, were popular with distillers and distributors of bourbon. Names such as *Cutter's Pure Bourbon, C. W. Wharton's Whiskey* and *Star Whiskey* are embossed on the bottles.

You could put together a substantial collection of handled whiskey jugs. However, prices are high, especially for early pontil-marked examples.

Figural whiskey bottles fall into several categories. The earliest examples were usually made with amber glass, but you may also find examples in green, aqua and yellow glass. These bottles resemble bitters bottles of the same period.

You will find them in a range of shapes and sizes, but many are relatively simple. For example, the Old Continental Whiskey bottle looks like a patent-medicine bottle except for its embossed columns and the likeness of a Continental soldier on one side. The spectacular examples include the Mohawk Pure Rye Whiskey bottle, which is in the form of an Indian princess. Incidentally, she closely resembles the maiden on the Brown's Celebrated Indian Herb Bitters bottle.

Other shapes from this period include Chicago Whiskey's barrel, and cannons for J. J. Gayen and Buchanan's Extract of Sugar Corn. W. & C. Co. of New York City featured a pineapple, and several different clocks appeared on Bininger's Regulator bottles. Some early versions of these pieces are pontil-marked.

Most of these containers are in fifth or quart sizes—until recently the standards for whiskeys. You may find a few examples of smaller bottles. Pints were seldom figural or elaborately embossed. Until late in the 19th century, only historical flasks in the pint size were deliberately designed to be attractive.

A rare exception is the round, yellow-amber pint bottle embossed with the busts of the 1892 Republican presidential and vice-presidential candidates. The embossing includes the slogan, *Our Choice/Cleve & Steve.* It

Milk glass was sometimes combined with white metal, or *spelter,* as in these two late-19th-century statuettes. Left: Statue of Liberty. Right: Christopher Columbus.

Among the most popular Jim Beam whiskey bottles are political figures. The Democratic donkey dates from 1968. Made in large numbers, these bottles have not increased greatly in value over the past decade.

referred to Grover Cleveland and his running mate Adlai E. Stevenson.

SAMPLERS

Small figural vessels, designed in most cases to be *samplers,* or *tasters,* were common. These were bottles containing samples of whiskey. They were given away by tavern owners and liquor dealers. Some samplers contained nearly a pint, but most held smaller amounts.

Most samplers were not heavily embossed, but they came in wonderful shapes. They looked like pistols, shoes, clamshells and even pigs. The pigs, in amber or clear glass, are especially appealing to collectors because they are usually heavily embossed.

One typical example was marked *Good Old Bourbon In A Hog's,* and another *Duffy's Crescent Saloon, Jefferson Street, Louisville, Ky.*

Some samplers featured subtle messages. One vessel was shaped like a shoe with a toe poking up through the broken leather. This was a graphic reminder of the fate that befell those who devoted too much time and money to the bottle. By contrast, some clear-glass, clock-shaped samplers carried a reminder, in bold black letters, that it was *Time to Take a Drink.*

Other small whiskey bottles were embossed, not with company names, but with slogans related to their contents. Two typical examples were marked *Traveler's Companion* and *Picnic.* These relatively common specimens are inexpensive and easy to find.

EUROPEAN FIGURALS

During the 1880s, a different type of bottle, known as the *European figural,* appeared on the American market. The intricate designs on these bottles were inspired by the technical quality and beautiful patterns of European glassmakers. The main influence came from the French and Germans.

These bottles were produced in both Europe and the United States. They usually contained imported liquors or brandies. Most were made with clear glass, but some were made with frosted or colored glass, including blue, green or red. Paint was sometimes added to highlight the design.

Many European figurals were in the form of political personalities, such as President Cleveland, or sports heroes, such as John L. Sullivan. Others reflected the interests of the people who drank the liquors—golfers, rowers and tennis players. These were not the types of activities popular with the hardy imbibers of the less-expensive domestic liquors.

There are also numerous figurals in white milk glass. Well-known examples include the squatting bear and the Atterbury duck. The latter is a duck that appears to be swallowing the bottle of which it is part. Even more interesting are bottles in the form of statues, such as the Statue of Liberty. In each case, the base is a white milk-glass bottle. The top is a figure cast in bronze or white metal.

Collector interest in these "European" types is not as great as the interest in American figural whiskey bottles. Even so, because the pieces were not made in great quantities, they can be expensive.

CONTEMPORARY WINE AND WHISKEY BOTTLES

One of the best areas for today's collector is in contemporary whiskey and wine bottles, such as the Jim Beam series. These bottles are often produced in small quantities, and the designs are changed every few years. Therefore, some may become quite valuable in a short period of time.

BUYING AND SELLING BEER, WINE AND WHISKEY BOTTLES

- The great majority of beer bottles were made only in amber. Look for bottles in other colors, such as green, aqua or red. Early pontil-marked beer bottles are also very desirable.
- Many breweries produced different types of bottles in several sizes, including half-pints, pints and quarts. Complete collections of these are interesting and valuable.
- Most wine bottles are found in amber, green or clear glass. Look for examples in teal, red, sea green and other unusual colors. A pontil mark also adds to the bottle's value.
- Most whiskey bottles are amber or dark green and have the same shape. The value of a whiskey bottle is often based on its embossed advertising. The famous Bininger bottles, and containers with the names of Kentucky bourbon distillers, are highly prized.
- Remember that liquor bottles with their original labels and contents are worth more than plain, empty bottles.
- Look for wine and whiskey bottles in dumps, especially those near old stores. Whiskey was sold in grocery stores until late in the 19th century. Also look near old hotels.
- Because most wine and whiskey bottles were made with dark glass, they are not usually as damaged or stained by burial in the ground as are aqua or clear-glass bottles.
- Figural whiskey bottles bring high prices—almost as much as comparable bitters bottles. Check price guides before you buy or sell these containers.
- Like all valuable figural bottles, the figural whiskey bottles you encounter may have been damaged and then cleverly repaired. Examine all these bottles under an ultraviolet light before you buy them.
- Remember that many figural whiskey and liquor bottles were made in Europe. These bottles do not bring the same prices as American bottles.
- Buy the new figural whiskeys—such as Jim Beam and Ezra Brooks—when they first appear in liquor stores. If you delay and have to buy them from a collector, you will have to pay a premium price.

INK BOTTLES

Ink bottles are among the most popular of all collectible bottles—and for good reasons. They come in many attractive shapes and colors, and they are small. Their size is a major consideration for the enthusiast who wants to amass a collection of several hundred specimens.

EARLY INK BOTTLES

Ink bottles were probably among the first bottles manufactured in this country. By 1772, Henry William Stiegel's glassworks in Manheim, Pennsylvania, was advertising "inks of all sorts." By 1800, these containers were made in many different forms.

Cone Designs—The earliest ink bottles were free-blown and labeled rather than embossed. Therefore, you will not be able to distinguish them from other small bottles. However, one basic form began to emerge in the 1870s—the *cone*. This is a round, squat bottle with a heavy base. It is wide at the bottom and tapers to a narrow top.

The cone is an ideal ink vessel because it concentrates most of the ink at the bottom. Therefore, it is not likely to tip over when a pen is inserted into it. Cone-form ink bottles are still made, and they are the most common form found in collections.

Other Designs—The *umbrella* ink bottle is similar to the cone. It has the same basic form, but instead of being round, it can have from 6 to 16 sides. The geometric forms of the umbrellas and the unusual hues in the glass make them very appealing.

You may come across both cone and umbrella ink vessels with pontil marks. These are especially valuable bottles. Also valuable are bottles bearing the embossed name of the manufacturer or seller. Embossing on these bottles was rare until the middle of the 19th century.

Another early and extremely desirable ink vessel is the *blown three-mold in geometric form*. Most were made before 1840 in New England. They are small, either circular or square, and come in dark shades. Their surfaces are covered with an embossed diamond pattern. Almost all are pontil-marked.

They are sometimes referred to as *Stoddard* or *Keene* inks because some think that many were made in those New Hampshire communities. Geometric ink bottles are prized not only by ink-bottle collectors, but also by general collectors of early American glass.

SCHOOLHOUSE INKS

After the Civil War, other molded forms appeared. Most common were the square or rectangular bottles with slightly sloping shoulders. They are often called *schoolhouse* inks. Bottles resemble small buildings, such as schoolhouses. Also, these bottles were often used in schoolrooms. You will find one or two indented ridges

Carter's master ink bottle, with gothic rib design. These attractive bottles were made at the turn of the century. They are relatively common.

across the front of many of these bottles. These ridges were used to hold pens. Schoolhouse ink bottles were usually made with clear or aqua glass. They are fairly easy to find today.

TURTLE AND TEAKETTLE INKS

You will have difficulty locating *turtle* and *teakettle* ink bottles. Turtle ink vessels are round, with a pouring spout at one side. They look somewhat like an igloo with a chimney—or a turtle. Teakettle ink bottles are usually eight-sided. They taper from the bottom toward the top and have a spout rising from the base at one side. The neck of the spout resembles that of a teakettle spout.

Both turtle and teakettle inks can be found in aqua or clear glass. However, one of their attractions for the serious collector is the great variety of other hues in

Master ink bottle with iron-pontil mark. Nearly a foot high, this green, 12-sided bottle was used for ink storage. Such containers are rare today.

which they are found. The colors include yellow, purple, blue, gray, green and red-amber. Turtle and teakettle ink containers in rare colors can be very expensive.

FIGURAL INKS

Figural ink bottles first appeared during the late 19th century. They were intended as a novelty to boost sales in a highly competitive market. They came in many shapes, ranging from bananas to houses. Among the most sought-after shapes are hats, shoes and boots. Almost all of these vessels were made with aqua or clear glass. The majority were made after 1870. As with all figural bottles, these pieces are expensive.

MASTER INKS

Ink bottles range in size from those holding only a fraction of an ounce to those holding a gallon. The majority of ink bottles are very small. However, you may come across pint, quart and gallon sizes.

These larger sizes, called *master inks*, were used for bulk transportation and bulk sale. Individual ink bottles could be taken to a stationery store and refilled from a master. Early master inks were mold-blown from green glass. They have a pouring spout and sometimes a pontil mark.

Later and more common examples are in aqua, blue or clear glass. Many of the later master inks are embossed with the name of a well-known ink manufacturer, such as *Carter* or *Stafford.* Carter examples are particularly appealing. They are embossed with gothic-arch patterns similar to those found on Victorian pickle bottles.

INKSTANDS

Inkstands are similar to ink bottles. Ink bottles were intended primarily for the storage and sale of ink, although they could also be used as inkwells. Inkstands served exclusively as wells. The inkstands best-known to collectors are circular glass vessels mounted on cast-iron frames. They are called *snails* because of their shape. Snails were made with clear glass and milk glass. They often bear late 19th-century patent marks.

Some very elaborate inkstands, including figural examples, were also made. Perhaps the most desirable of these is one that represents the Memorial Hall at the Philadelphia Exposition of 1876. It is made of pressed glass and is designed to accommodate ink, pens and blotting material. This particular example is embossed with the name of the moldmaker who designed it.

Unfortunately, many of these complex inkstands are found damaged. Small glass corners and protuberances are easily broken off. Avoid purchasing a broken sample unless the price is a fraction of the value of a similar piece in good condition.

COLLECTING INK BOTTLES

Many varieties of inkwells and ink bottles exist, but few are readily available. You will have no trouble finding square or rectangular bottles, especially in aqua, clear or amber glass. Cones are also easy to locate. However, other forms and unusual colors are difficult to find and are expensive.

Bottle dealers often stock rarer types of ink bottles. You may find some rare examples at bottle shows. Also look for ink-collectors' clubs, whose specialized publications provide an opportunity to advertise for choice pieces. If you search diligently, you can sometimes come across ink vessels in out-of-the-way storage places.

Books and exhibitions have led to increased interest in ink vessels. Therefore, these bottles are becoming more difficult to find.

Clear-glass inkstand, representing the Memorial Hall erected for the Philadelphia Centennial of 1876. Marked with the name of the moldmaker, this piece is of interest to collectors of both ink bottles and centennial items.

BUYING AND SELLING INK BOTTLES

• The factors that affect the value of an ink bottle are form, color, the presence of an embossed maker's name and a pontil mark.

• Because most ink bottles were small, larger pieces command better prices. The value of a bottle is also enhanced if it has a pouring lip.

• Early geometric ink vessels came in various patterns and designs. Some are much rarer than others. Study specialized books on ink bottles, so you can recognize rare examples. They are sometimes worth 10 times as much as an almost identical piece in a common pattern.

• Because of the almost universal use of the ball-point pen, ink is rarely sold in bottles today. Contemporary ink bottles are, therefore, increasing in value. These bottles are still readily available, so you can be particular in your selection. Choose only examples in good condition with original labels.

• Among the most common ink bottles are cone styles made during the late 19th and early 20th centuries. Most of these bottles were in aqua, clear or amber glass. You can put together a good collection of these inexpensively. Watch for examples made in rarer colors, such as yellow, red and emerald green.

• Inkstands had several parts, usually including a metal frame and one or two glass wells. A complete inkstand is hard to find. It is easier and much less expensive to buy individual parts and make up a matching set yourself.

• Figural ink bottles are rare. Most were made with aqua or clear glass, so examples in other colors are even more valuable. Pontiled examples in colored glass are especially desirable.

• Never remove a paper label from an ink bottle. It contributes to the bottle's value. If a bottle still contains ink, do not throw the ink away. It, too, increases the worth of the container.

BARBER, PERFUME AND COLOGNE BOTTLES

Among the more unusual bottles available to collectors are barber, perfume and cologne bottles. Although interesting to many collectors, they are not widely stocked by dealers. If you decide to collect these bottles, you will have to sharpen your bottle-hunting skills.

BARBER BOTTLES

Barber bottles reflect a period of American history when the barbershop was essentially a men's club. Many gentlemen went to the barbershop each day to have a beard trim. The barbering might take only a few minutes, but reading the newspaper and socializing could stretch the time to hours.

During the second half of the 19th century, it became customary for regular clients to have their own sets of bottles. These personalized bottles served as a sanitary measure and as part of the barbershop ritual. The bottles held various liquids—such as witch hazel, cologne and bay rum—used by the barber.

Most barber bottles have round or oval bodies and long necks. Many have a pewter top. Necks may be decorated with rings of applied glass, or they may be gently curved or fluted. These bottles have distinctive colors and decorations. Barber bottles are among the most colorful and elaborate of all bottles.

Barber bottles appear in a wide variety of opaque and translucent shades. You will find examples in blue, green, red, amber and orange; and in blue, white and black milk glass. Color is only part of the decoration. There are few examples in clear glass.

Free-blown examples are sometimes embellished with hand-painted designs, either floral or figural. The best-known of the figurals are the *Mary Gregory* decorations. These are pictures of children, painted in white on cobalt-blue glass. The original pictures of this type are often credited to a famous glass decorator named Mary Gregory, who worked at the Sandwich, Massachusetts, glass factory in the late 19th century. However, many bottles bearing these designs were made at other glassworks, including many factories in central Europe.

American companies that made barber bottles included the Sandwich Glass Co. and the New England Glass Bottle Co., both in Massachusetts, and Hobbs, Brockunier & Co. in West Virginia.

Most barber bottles were made in Europe and were imported in the late 19th century. Very few of these bottles were marked or otherwise identified, so collectors acquire whatever pleases them. There is no way that you can limit your collection according to origin or place of manufacture.

Milk-glass barber bottles from the late 19th century. Each has a lithographed picture of a woman and the owner's name set under a clear-glass cover.

Cologne or fire-extinguisher bottle in white milk-glass, 1890 to 1910. These bottles are also found in clear glass, usually with painted and gilded decorations.

ART-GLASS BARBER BOTTLES

Most barber bottles were made at a time when large glassmaking companies in the United States and Europe were perfecting *art glass*. The term encompasses numerous types of colorful glass, many of which were used for barber bottles.

Some bottles were made with *hobnail glass,* which was covered with a knoblike pattern. Others were made with *candy-stripe glass.* You can easily recognize this type. It consists of thin strands of white against a contrasting background. Some bottles were made with *vasa murrhina,* a varicolored glass with silver or gold metallic flecks. These and other art-glass designs make the field of barber bottles both beautiful and challenging.

COLLECTING BARBER BOTTLES

All types that have been discussed are collectible. However, many collectors look for bottles that have the names of contents printed on them. These bottles carry words such as *Hair Tonic, Vegederma* or *Bay Rum* in attractive letters.

Even more highly prized are bottles that have the names or initials of the original owners on them. In most cases, the names or initials were lettered onto the bottle's surface. On some interesting examples, however, the name was printed in black or gold letters on a small oval piece of paper. This paper was fitted behind a removable piece of clear glass. These examples are called *name plates.* They are especially valuable if accompanied by a printed picture of a young woman.

Barber bottles were made from about 1850 until 1920. They appear on the sales lists of many American and European glass factories. Even so, they are not common today. Examples sometimes show up among collections of art glass offered by antique dealers. Specialized bottle dealers sometimes stock them, too.

If you become a serious collector, however, you will have to look further. Most of your acquisitions will have to come from trades with other collectors or through advertising. These bottles were seldom discarded intact, so you cannot expect to find them by digging at old sites.

PERFUME AND COLOGNE BOTTLES

Perfume and cologne bottles are usually less spectacular than barber bottles. However, in their day, they were more important. Until the late 19th century, most people didn't bathe very often. They lacked hot water, indoor plumbing and our concern for personal hygiene. Perfume and cologne helped make social life a little more tolerable.

American glassworks such as Henry William Stie-

Barber bottles in hobnail glass with pewter stoppers. These bottles were probably made in Europe.

gel's factory in Manheim, Pennsylvania, produced perfume and cologne bottles during the 1770s. They also made small containers for smelling salts. Because perfume was very strong, it was sold in small containers.

Stiegel bottles held about a half-pint and were shaped like a flattened globe with a short neck. They were mold-blown to produce ribbed or diamond patterns. These bottles are found in lovely colors, including amethyst, blue, sapphire, puce and yellow.

Stiegel bottles are rare and expensive. Unfortunately, they are often difficult to distinguish from reproductions and contemporary European containers. You should purchase a piece only when you are offered a written guarantee of the bottle's authenticity.

Designs—The design of perfume bottles has varied over the years. Most bottles made during the 19th century were round and plain. Perfumes made in the late 19th and early 20th centuries were often figural and beautifully embossed.

Bottles produced from about 1910 to 1925 were much less intricate. They were usually round or octagonal and had little decoration. Vessels manufactured from about 1925 to 1940 were often designed more like their turn-of-the-century counterparts. They came in many shapes and colors.

Since 1940, perfume bottles have again become less interesting. The bottles are usually round and seldom have much embossing.

COLOGNE BOTTLES

Because cologne is perfume diluted with alcohol, more is required to gain the desired effect. For this reason, cologne containers were usually larger than those for perfumes.

You will probably come across many plain cologne bottles, including early aqua examples with pontil marks. These bottles resemble medicine bottles and can be recognized only if the original label is present.

There are also some lovely, long-necked bottles in various shades of milk glass. These bottles are frequently attributed to the Sandwich, Massachusetts, glassworks.

For the majority of collectors, the most desirable cologne bottles are figural. These bottles are usually 4- to 7-inches high and made with clear or aqua glass. They come in hundreds of shapes. The most common forms are floral, with trees, leaflike scrolls or baskets of flowers embossed on the surface. Sometimes the entire piece resembles a basket of flowers.

Figural colognes were also made in various human forms. These include court jesters, crying babies, women in winter coats with muffs, and dapper gentlemen. Many of these pieces were produced by American glassworks in the 1830s and bear pontil marks. Many early examples have survived. You are certain to be delighted if you come across any of these beautiful pieces.

Colognes were so popular that a desperate family once had one made in an attempt to locate a missing son. In 1874, a young man named Charlie Ross was abducted by strangers. After seeking him in vain for several years, his family commissioned a glass factory to emboss his likeness on a cologne bottle. The family hoped that someone using the bottle might recognize the boy. Sad to say, the attempt failed. The so-called *Charlie Ross* cologne bottle is a very popular collectible.

COLLECTING PERFUME AND COLOGNE BOTTLES

Early perfume bottles and figural colognes are eagerly sought and have become rather expensive. The majority of these bottles are owned by collectors and bottle dealers. The best examples can be obtained from these sources.

Even so, colognes were frequently kept by their original owners because of their attractiveness. Sometimes a family that has occupied the same home for many years has amassed some excellent examples. Try advertising in a local newspaper for bottles you want. You may be surprised at the result.

Avon perfume bottle in the form of a hot-fudge sundae, 1975 to 1980. Like all Avon bottles, this quaint piece is certain to increase in value.

HAIR PREPARATIONS

Our Victorian ancestors were as concerned about hair care as we are. Falling hair, split ends and dandruff were as troublesome 100 years ago as they are today. Manufacturers were glad to provide a variety of solutions for these problems. If hair looked dull and listless, Burt's Hair Reviver would perk it up. If it wasn't long enough, you bought Seven Sutherland Sisters Hair Grower. It may even have worked—all of the sisters had hair down to their ankles. They also had $3 million, all earned by the family concoction during the 38 years it was on the market.

COLLECTING HAIR PREPARATIONS

Bottles for many different hair renewers and tonics are easy to find. You can amass an interesting collection of preparations, such as Ayer's Hair Vigor, World's Hair Restorer and Dr. Tebbett's Physiological Hair Regenerator. Related collectibles include hair-tonic bottles. The tonic was designed to keep unruly locks in place. You can also find hair-dye bottles.

Perfume bottles in cut or pressed glass, 1920 to 1940. These attractive bottles are drawing increasing attention from collectors.

Most hair-preparation bottles were made with aqua or clear glass. They are interesting for their embossing and the labels that some still bear. A few types, such as Hall's Hair Restorer, came in lovely green, blue or violet hues.

Figural forms were not common. A notable and attractive exception was the bottle made for the hair tonic produced by John Hart & Co. Appropriately enough, this bottle was heart-shaped. It was of amber glass.

Most hair renewers and tonics came in plain rectangular, square or round bottles. Most are easy to find and cost relatively little. You can find them at dumps or old storage areas because once the contents had been used, there was little reason to save the bottles. They were thrown away.

BUYING AND SELLING BARBER AND COLOGNE BOTTLES

• Many barber bottles have gilded or enameled decoration. Avoid examples on which this decoration has worn off. Such pieces are not as valuable as those in better condition.

• Because so many barber bottles were pontil-marked, the presence of such a mark will not usually increase the value.

• Some barber bottles have been copied. New pieces are made of thicker glass and lack pontil marks. Also, they do not show the signs of wear found on earlier bottles, especially on bases.

• A set of several barber bottles with matching decorations or designs will be worth more than an equal number of unrelated examples.

• Try to find cologne bottles made with colored glass. Most of these vessels were made with clear glass, so a colored one will bring a higher price.

• Do not be concerned if your cologne or barber bottle was made in Europe. Most were, but they are just as valuable as those made in the United States.

• A cologne bottle with an original paper label is uncommon. Such labels should never be removed. Their presence will increase the value of a bottle 100% or more.

• Bottles that contained hair tonic, blacking or hair-growth preparations are readily available and are usually inexpensive. Unlike barber and cologne bottles, many of these containers were thrown away. Look for them in dumps, cellars and attics. The best examples are those made with blue, red or green glass.

• Several hair-tonic bottles have been copied. New ones are made with bright-purple, red or sapphire-blue glass. These colors are very different from those used for earlier examples.

• Never discard the pewter or tin pouring spout sometimes found on a barber or hair-tonic bottle. It is an original part of the bottle, adding to the value of the piece.

MISCELLANEOUS BOTTLES

Most bottle collectors concentrate on the types of bottles we have discussed. However, many enthusiasts are interested in other kinds. Some of these bottles, such as drug, poison and snuff containers, are similar to bottles you are familiar with. Others, such as target balls and fire extinguishers, are very different.

DRUG BOTTLES

This category includes numerous types of containers. They were used to store solid, powdered or liquid medicinal preparations used by druggists and doctors.

Some bottles had wide mouths and were intended to hold powders or lumpy materials. Some had narrow necks and were designed for liquids. All had stoppers. Some had ground-glass stoppers. Most had corks.

Many of these bottles were made with inexpensive aqua, green or amber glass. Some later examples were made with clear glass. A few drug bottles were made with high-quality crystal or artificially colored glass. Colored-glass examples are often called *show bottles*. They were sometimes displayed in shop windows. Many had elaborate, gold-and-black labels.

The earliest drug bottles had either open- or iron-pontil marks. These containers are highly prized. They are particularly valuable if they are embossed with the name and address of a druggist—or *chemist,* as they were often called. Cobalt blue or deep-green bottles are particular favorites with collectors.

Of lesser interest and therefore more reasonably priced are aqua or amber bottles bearing the embossed name of a druggist or a paper label listing contents. Some of the drug names printed on the labels sound exotic today. Among the more peculiar were *podophyllin* and *cincho quinine.* As with other bottles, labels on drug bottles should be preserved. They enhance a bottle's interest and value.

POISON BOTTLES

Poison bottles are similar to drug bottles. During the 19th century, it was customary to keep poisons in the home. Most poisons were used to control rodents and other pests, and were sold by grocers and druggists. The danger of home-storage of these concoctions was recognized. Elaborate bottles were designed to prevent accidental use or poisonings.

Most poison bottles were marked *Poison* in large letters. In 1829, New York State made such marking mandatory. However, many people could not read. In homes lit by candles or oil lamps, it was often hard to make out the words even if you *could* read.

By the middle of the 19th century, bottle factories

Poison bottles, 1900 to 1910. Poison bottles are easy to identify. They usually come in cobalt blue and have a rough texture on tops and sides. Many have sharp points on tops, making it unlikely that they would be mistaken for something else, even in the dark.

had developed special bottles for poisons. The surfaces of these bottles were covered with sharp knobs or ridges. Even in the dark, the feel of such an unusual bottle would alert the user.

Some manufacturers went further, making their bottles in the form of a coffin or putting a prominent skull-and-crossbones symbol on them. The bottles were intended as gruesome reminders of the consequences of misuse. These figural bottles are now the most popular and costly of all poison containers.

In 1872, the American Medical Association (AMA) recommended the use of colored-glass poison bottles. Makers responded by turning out blue, green and amber bottles. Blue seems to have been the most common color and is the most popular among collectors.

Poison bottles are also distinguished by shape. Some are triangular, a very unusual shape for a bottle. Sometimes the bottles had unusual closures. A few bottles had tops covered with sharp points. It was impossible to remove these tops without being aware of the nature of the container. Later bottles had safety closures—much like the closures on modern medicine bottles—that were meant to prevent children from opening the bottles.

COLLECTING DRUG AND POISON BOTTLES

Poison bottles are popular with collectors because of their novelty. Some collectors enjoy their somewhat gruesome associations and some enjoy their unusual forms. Because only about 200 American types exist, it is not difficult to gather a fairly comprehensive collection.

You should not confuse drug bottles with poison bottles. Although the bottles are similar, collecting one type is not like collecting the other. Drug bottles are common and readily available, usually at low prices. You can often get them in quantity when old drugstores close. Drug bottles are usually part of the inventory of every bottle dealer.

This is not the case with poison bottles. You will find that collector interest is greater, so far fewer bottles are available. Blue and figural examples are especially coveted. In fact, you should not be surprised to find a figural poison bottle going for hundreds of dollars. You will find very few poison bottles in dumps or attics. Focus your attention on bottle shows and specialized collectors' clubs.

SNUFF AND BLACKING BOTTLES

Snuff is the powdered, and sometimes scented, tobacco widely used during the 19th century. It was shipped and sold in rectangular bottles having pontil marks. Blacking for shoes and other leather goods was packed in round or square bottles. Snuff bottles and blacking bottles are usually grouped together by

Drug bottles, 1890 to 1910. Drug bottles came in various sizes and colors, including blue and amber. Tops were usually mushroom-shaped and fit into the necks of the bottles, which were ground to ensure a snug fit. The glass cap on the bottle third from left was intended to hold one dose of medicine.

Fire-extinguisher bottle in the form of a tenpin, 1880 to 1900. The presence of the original sealed top and contents increases the value of this unusual piece.

collectors. Both are approximately the same size.

The most interesting examples of snuff and blacking bottles are pontil-marked and made with amber, dark green or black glass. Both snuff and blacking bottles sometimes have embossing or paper labels. The embossing or a label greatly increases a bottle's value.

Snuff and blacking bottles are usually small. However, one late-19th-century snuff manufacturer, George W. Helme, used large amber containers. These bottles looked like canning or fruit jars and were used for shipping.

COLLECTING SNUFF AND BLACKING BOTTLES

These collectibles are considered desirable by many, so they bring good prices. You can find them at quality bottle shows and in the shops of specialized dealers. Both types are sturdy—and are likely to be found in good condition in dumps and other excavations. Because they were made with dark-hued glass, the color seldom turned milky due to exposure to moisture. Subtler colors would turn milky.

FIRE-EXTINGUISHER BOTTLES

Fire extinguishers—or *fire-extinguisher bottles,* as they are often called—were once made of glass. Most were heavy glass balls, with either long or short necks. They were filled with a carbon-tetrachloride mixture. In case of fire, a ball was thrown directly into the flames, where it broke and produced a fire-smothering foam.

The first fire extinguisher of this sort was patented in 1863. Many different shapes were produced during the next 40 years. Fire extinguishers were made in the shape of beer kegs, dumbbells and perfume bottles. Most extinguishers were aqua, but some were blue, green, yellow, amber or red. The bottles were usually stored in groups of three in a wire rack, but some were hung from chains.

COLLECTING FIRE-EXTINGUISHER BOTTLES

Fire extinguishers are collected by a small but enthusiastic group. Prices are fairly high. But because the bottles are relatively unknown, you may be able to find a bargain. Colored bottles and those with original holders, contents and paper labels are the most valuable. These pieces rarely appear at auctions. You are more likely to find them at specialized bottle shows. Occasionally, collectors find them in old houses. Don't forget to advertise—firefighting buffs sometimes have collections, too.

TARGET BALLS

Target balls are hollow, glass spheres, 2 to 3 inches in diameter. Although they aren't bottles, they are eagerly sought by bottle collectors.

Open-pontil snuff bottle marked *By A.A. Cooley, Hartford,* 1825 to 1845. This is a rare piece. Very few early snuff and blacking bottles are marked.

Fire-extinguisher bottle in the form of a light bulb, early 20th century. This bottle fits into a metal sling marked *Shur Stop.* Because it has the original contents and the sling, this bottle is particularly valuable.

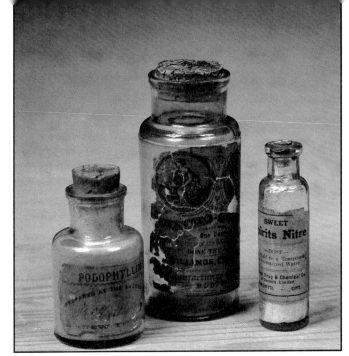

Labeled druggists' bottles made from 1870 to 1900 are reasonably priced. Labels list some interesting ingredients, such as podophyllin, sweet spirits nitrite and cincho quinine.

Target balls were designed for shooting practice. Originally, hunters sharpened their skills on live pigeons. Public disapproval and the inconvenience of such targets for indoor shooting led to the development of blown-glass balls. These hollow balls could be filled with smoke, ribbons or confetti.

First produced in England during the 1830s, target balls were manufactured in the United States by 1850. The target-shooting feats of Buffalo Bill and Annie Oakley greatly increased interest in the sport. Target balls were made in great numbers until replaced in the 1880s and 1890s by the clay pigeon.

The balls come in several colors, including aqua, amber, blue and green. Their surface may be embossed with patterns of small raised dots or with gridlike arrangements. Some bear the embossed names of manufacturers or sellers. One example is marked *Ira Paine's Filled Ball Pat Oct 23 1877*. This is a well-known collectible.

Because target balls were made to be broken, they are difficult to find. They bring fairly high prices, especially if they are embossed or in a choice color, such as blue. You should look for them at bottle shows and in advertisements in bottle-club magazines.

LIGHTNING-ROD BALLS

Lightning-rod balls certainly are not bottles either—but they too are popular with bottle collectors. These hollow-glass spheres are 4 to 5 inches in diameter. They were designed to ornament lightning rods placed on rural homes and barns during the late 19th and early 20th centuries. One ball or more was usu-ally placed about a third of the way up on each metal rod. Even today, you can still see these brightly colored spheres on buildings throughout the eastern and midwestern United States.

Most lightning-rod balls were made with clear, amethyst or aqua glass. Some particularly attractive examples were made with blue or white milk glass. Some of the balls are embossed. They may be decorated with diamond patterns, stars, crescents or sunbursts.

Plain types of lightning-rod balls are readily available at modest prices. More elaborate examples are sought by specialized collectors. These rarer types bring substantial prices. Also look for lightning-rod balls at bottle shows and auctions. In addition, one of the best places to look for them is in the countryside. Some of the finest examples are still on rooftops, and you can occasionally buy them from farmers. Or, you can just drive by and enjoy their beauty and contribution to American glassmaking.

BUYING AND SELLING MISCELLANEOUS BOTTLES

- Some unusual types of vessels, such as fire-extinguisher bottles, are frequently not recognized by the average collector or dealer. Look for these in antique shops that usually don't carry many bottles. Also look for them at house and church sales. You can sometimes find a real bargain.
- Fire-extinguisher balls were often kept in racks or holders made of wire or metal. A group of balls in the proper holder is worth more than a group of individual balls.
- Druggists' bottles can often be purchased at very reasonable prices when an old-time drugstore closes. Old medicine bottles may be available, too. Never pass up the opportunity to attend an auction at such a store.
- Poison bottles with original contents are of interest to collectors. However, they are potentially very dangerous. Keep them where they cannot be reached by children or unsuspecting adults.
- Most poison bottles made with green glass were made in England. Most examples in blue or amber glass were manufactured in the United States.
- The tops to drug and poison bottles can be important. Many were made to fit a specific type of bottle. Buy extra tops whenever you can.
- Most snuff and blacking bottles were identified only by a paper label, and most of these labels have disappeared. As a result, embossed examples are particularly valuable. They bring even higher prices than pontil-marked snuff and blacking bottles.
- Remember that few people collect miscellaneous bottle types. Few dealers keep an extensive supply of examples. However, you can often find what you are looking for by advertising, talking with other collectors and contacting collectors' clubs.

Building a Collection

As you may have surmised, the number of bottles available to a collector is huge. The number of active collectors is also large and increasing every day. It is hardly surprising, then, that there are many ways to approach this hobby.

How *you* decide to collect bottles is a matter of personal taste. You can collect everything that comes your way, or you can specialize in one particular type of bottle. You can study your bottles and attempt to learn all you can about them and their makers, or you can choose to do nothing more than admire the beauty of your acquisitions.

There is no right or wrong way to go about establishing a collection. The right way is what gives you the most enjoyment. But because bottle collecting is such a vast field, the beginner can become confused. The following suggestions are intended to help you direct your collecting.

COLLECTING BY CATEGORY

As described in the previous chapter, early-American bottles can be divided into various collecting categories. Some of these are based on what the bottles originally contained.

Each category is large. For example, even if you specialize in medicines, you are still faced with a formidable array of bottles. Thousands of different bottles are available in this category. Accordingly, you may choose to confine your activities even further. As a collector of medicine bottles, you might seek only those bottles labeled or marked *Cure* or *Tonic*.

Another way to limit your collection is to acquire only pontil-marked examples in a single category. It would be difficult to add to your collection with any frequency, but the collection would be rare and interesting.

OVERLAPPING CATEGORIES

Categories often overlap, and you might choose to collect one type of bottle that can be found in several categories. For example, you might choose to collect only figural bottles. You would not necessarily be concerned with what the bottles once contained. Eventually, your collection might include poison, bitters, cologne and whiskey figurals. Such a collection can be very attractive.

You can also collect by color. Identical or similar colors appear in many different categories. You might choose to seek dark-blue or emerald-green bottles, and no others. Such a collection could include everything from milk bottles to canning jars.

COLLECTING BY PERIOD

Another way to limit your collection is to confine yourself to a particular period, such as the first half of the 19th century. If you do that, you would be collecting some of the earliest bottles available. A collection from this era would include bottles for whiskey, bitters and medicines. It would also include historical flasks, canning jars, ink bottles and even oddities such as target balls.

LIMITING YOUR COLLECTION

The categories discussed are only some of the possibilities. As you attend shows, read books and talk with other collectors, you will probably develop your own categories. To make bottle collecting more fun, consider the following basic guidelines:

Size of Category—Don't choose categories that are either too broad or too narrow. For example, a collection of whiskey bottles would be overwhelming. Thousands of varieties are available. Even if you had the space to store or display such a multitude, you would soon be disappointed. Most whiskey bottles look very much alike, and even a few hundred look very boring when displayed.

Sheer volume of a collection can restrict your enjoyment. It can also be difficult to do the necessary research to learn about the uses and origins of the pieces. This research is something that many collectors find fascinating. You will get more pleasure out of your collection if it is small enough for you to know and understand each bottle.

Don't be too specialized, however. If you decide to collect only umbrella-shaped, pontiled ink bottles, you won't have much fun. Such a collection is so specialized that months or even years might pass between acquisitions.

You might want to concentrate on a category-within-a-category, such as pictorial flasks.

Among the more challenging collections would be one that focused on such rarities as lightning-rod balls.

Cost—Don't forget to consider cost when choosing a category. Historical flasks, most figural whiskey and bitters bottles, and certain other bottles are generally quite expensive. It is a matter of supply and demand. Many collectors actively seek these pieces, and not enough are available to go around.

Unless you have sufficient money to spend, avoid categories already crowded with knowledgeable and wealthy collectors. Seek a relatively untouched area. You might decide to begin your collection with early 20th-century machine-made bottles or with food bottles. These categories offer a lot of bottles and have limited appeal.

History—If you enjoy history, bottle collecting can be a source of great interest. If you want to know more about the history of your city or town, for instance, you might collect bottles embossed with local names. You can probably locate containers with the names of druggists, whiskey dealers or grocers. You can do research about these bottles in your neighborhood library. You can learn a great deal about local history this way, and the research will add to your appreciation of acquisitions.

Factory Products—You might decide to collect only the bottles made by a specific glass factory. This is a challenging way to limit your collection. Your greatest problem will be that few glassworks placed their names on their products. Although these collections are difficult to assemble, they become quite valuable in time.

KEEPING VALUE IN MIND

Most collectors don't start collecting as an investment. Their acquisitions are a source of different satisfaction. Nevertheless, most bottles increase in value over the years. The rarer and more desirable examples appreciate more rapidly than ordinary bottles.

Quality vs. Quantity—When you have decided upon a category, try to obtain the best examples you can afford. These usually include the rarest, most attractive, most sought-after bottles. As a general rule, it is better to buy one bottle worth $10 than 10 worth $1 each.

The same rule applies to the condition of the bottles. Most damaged bottles are worth far less than comparable undamaged specimens. Don't let an inexpensive cracked or repaired bottle tempt you. Purchase a damaged bottle only if the piece is so rare that you may never see another.

Prune your collection from time to time. No matter what category you choose, you will probably start with many ordinary bottles and a few good ones. Over the years, your goal should be to replace the more common, less desirable examples with more choice specimens.

Most knowledgeable collectors prefer quality to

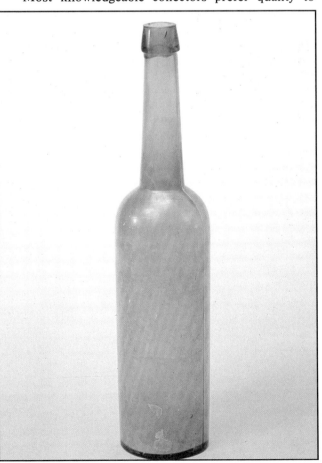

Look carefully for imperfections in a bottle. They always decrease its value. Even tiny chips or cracks will affect value, so be sure to examine expensive bottles with a magnifying glass. An ultraviolet light can reveal imperfections that might not be otherwise visible. The defects in this bottle occurred during the glassmaking process.

This was originally an aqua bottle. Dampness or underground burial made it turn yellowish. The bottle has also acquired an iridescent, scaly surface. This condition cannot be reversed.

When choosing a category of bottles to collect, consider how much you can afford. Flasks such as these cost as much as $1,000 each. Flasks are rare and popular among collectors.

quantity. They are more interested in having 100 wonderful medicine bottles than 500 mediocre ones. Trade or sell your less valuable bottles to finance or make room for new acquisitions.

FINDING BOTTLES

You can get bottles from many sources—some better than others. One important source is yourself. You can find some bottles at no cost, through your own work and ingenuity. One way is to dig. This is probably the most popular way of getting old bottles in rural areas—and sometimes in cities, too.

Old bottles were discarded in various ways. Many empty containers were simply thrown into the local trash dump. Some were pitched down old wells that were being filled. Others were hidden under the floorboards of barns or dropped down privies by guilt-ridden

You may get a chance to buy bottles from a grocery store or drugstore that is going out of business. If you do, be sure to look for old advertising and promotional pieces that went with the bottles. A bottle with pertinent advertising material will bring a higher price than a bottle without.

Building a Collection 63

drinkers. Some were buried under debris when buildings burned down.

Considering the punishment old bottles have endured, it is surprising that they have survived in such great numbers. Many have been damaged, of course. Some have suffered deterioration—natural hues have been replaced by a milky appearance through exposure to dampness. But many bottles emerge from the ground looking almost as bright and new as they did originally.

Digging for bottles is like a treasure hunt. It can be profitable and exciting. Following are a few simple rules you should follow.

DIGGING FOR BOTTLES

The first step is to get permission to enter the property you want to explore. This applies to all property, including abandoned houses, old barns or big-city excavations. No matter how desolate the property may appear, assume that it is owned by someone. If you enter someone else's property without permission, you are trespassing. If you remove something from that property, you are stealing.

Always be careful. Watch out for natural dangers. Depending upon the area, these may include sunstroke, cave-ins, quicksand or rattlesnakes. Always wear heavy gloves and strong shoes. Sharp objects, including broken glass and jagged pieces of metal, are common in dumps and garbage pits.

If you follow these simple precautions, digging is safe and enjoyable.

LOCATING SITES

Locating likely sites can be difficult. One reason is that many old dumps and similar places are no longer recognizable as such. Look for old houses, cellar holes and other signs of former habitation. Not far away, there's likely to be an old dump.

Farms—Old farms are also excellent places to look. Be sure to check the areas near barns and other buildings. You should also look in deep hollows or valleys near the main house. It was always convenient to dump things down a steep slope.

Often, a dump will be indicated only by a few rusted pieces of iron or by broken glass. Don't let this fool you. A treasure trove may lie just a few feet beneath the surface. Consider using a metal detector. Where there is metal, there is often a dump.

When you become accustomed to the layout of old farms, you will develop a knack for spotting good places to dig. It takes some practice.

Old houses, sheds and barns merit investigation, too. Many people saved old bottles to use or sell. These were stored either in outbuildings or storage spaces such as cellars, attics, lofts and crawl spaces. Look everywhere in an old building—under the eaves and in cabinets, closets and wardrobes. You may even find bottles under beds, as some collectors have. Bottles stored in houses have been protected from the weather and are likely to be in better condition than those from dumps.

Using Maps—When you are looking for dumps and old structures, it often pays to use topographical maps of the area. These maps show early roads and dwellings. Many topographical maps have not been revised since the 1920s. They can be an excellent source of information, revealing the locations of old structures that might otherwise be difficult to find.

Like treasure hunting, digging through dumps and rummaging through old buildings is an uncertain thing. It can produce some real finds, or it can result in nothing but poison ivy, mosquito bites and bumped heads.

But for many collectors, it's the most satisfying way of collecting bottles. If you acquire your containers by digging for them, your collection will be very special. Each bottle you find will have its own tale. You will have the satisfying feeling of rescuing some Americana from obscurity.

DIVING FOR BOTTLES

Underwater bottle collecting calls for special skills. To hunt for bottles underwater, you should be an experienced scuba diver. Like all diving, this work takes skill. Don't do it without adequate equipment and expert guidance.

The first such explorers started looking for sunken ships off the Florida and California coasts. In the early 1960s, they began probing the depths of canals in New York state and Pennsylvania. These explorations have proven surprisingly successful, especially for collectors who concentrate on areas near canal locks. Barges were often delayed for long periods near these locks. Used bottles were simply tossed into the water. The sites of old taverns or hotels along canals are also good places to look.

BUYING AND BARTERING

Some collectors tend to get most of their bottles by searching in old buildings and dumps. Others acquire much of their collections through buying or bartering.

If you choose to buy, you can seek bottles from various sources. Antique shops often carry bottles; so do secondhand stores. There are also specialized bottle dealers. Some have their own shops; others organize shows or sell through the mail. Bottle specialists often advertise in the magazines and newsletters devoted to the hobby.

Advertise—If you find that local antique shops and shows don't offer enough bottles, you can do a little advertising yourself. A few advertisements in bottle journals will usually result in numerous offers. Be specific in your ad—a request for "old bottles" doesn't tell people enough. Explain that you are looking for specific types—such as old soda or medicine bottles.

Another good place to find bottles is in old sheds and outbuildings. Since they will be sheltered from the weather here, the bottles will often have original labels, like the ones this lucky collector is examining.

Displaying bottles against a window allows light to shine through them, showing their shapes and colors well. With this type of display, keep the window closed at all times. It's a good idea to attach bottles to the window ledge with double-stick tape. Be sure to use tape that will not form a permanent bond.

Plexiglas shelves allow viewers to see the bottles from all sides.

Wood shelves can hold a large collection. The shelves shown here, which belong to a prominent collector, have been carefully arranged and lighted from the back.

If you are adventurous, you might try running notices in local newspapers. You can also post your requests in grocery stores or post offices. Many excellent old bottles have been acquired this way.

Remember that when you advertise in non-specialist media such as newspapers and shops, you are not specifically addressing bottle collectors. This may waste some of your efforts. Most people who read the notice won't know what you are looking for.

Auctions—Don't forget about auctions. Many auction houses occasionally include flasks or bottles in their sales. If so, this is a chance to find a bargain. Desirable bottles sometimes slip by without being noticed by collectors or bottle dealers, so you have an opportunity to get them at very low prices.

Every so often, auctions are devoted primarily or exclusively to bottles. The expertise at these auctions is another matter. When desirable pieces are offered, major dealers and collectors will either be there or will be represented by agents. Any bottle that goes for a low price at such a sale is probably common or has serious flaws.

Even so, such an auction is good training for a beginner. You can meet notable collectors, see how experts evaluate the bottles offered, and watch how these people bid.

Auctioned bottles that are part of an important collection are sometimes more valuable than similar pieces that are not. Remember that a bottle auctioned is usually no different than one you can get in a shop. Don't get carried away by the sense of competition or by the desire to own something from a major collection.

Before the bidding starts, you should know what a bottle is worth and what you are willing to pay for it. When you reach your limit, stop bidding. Most people who pay too much at an auction have only themselves to blame.

Never bid on anything you have not previously examined during the viewing. Auctioneers have no obligation to tell you what is wrong with a bottle. Usually, they will, but in many cases they may not even know.

You can also obtain bottles through the closing or sale of old businesses, particularly drugstores or grocery stores. Many of these stores have been in business for decades. As newer products became available, obsolete medicine or food bottles were often stored and forgotten. Many desirable, labeled bottles with original contents—prized by advanced collectors—have been found this way.

SELLING YOUR BOTTLES

As your collection grows, you will probably want to sell some of your bottles. You may want to replace common examples with better pieces. Or, your interests may change, and you may wish to get rid of examples you no longer want.

You can sell bottles through the same outlets you use to buy them. These include dealers, auctions and newsletters. There are some simple rules you should follow:

Never sell a bottle without knowing what it is and what it is worth. Just because a bottle doesn't interest you doesn't mean it isn't valuable. Always check the value of a bottle through a price guide, such as the one included in this book. If you have questions, you may want to consult one—or perhaps several—reputable experts.

No sale is pure profit. If you sell at auction, you will have to pay the auction house a commission. This can be 10% to 20% of the price, and covers the overhead involved in arranging the sale.

If you sell to a dealer, remember that he has to make a profit, too. A dealer will pay you no more than 50% to 70% of the retail value of the piece. Only through a direct private sale to another collector can you hope to receive anything close to the book value of a bottle.

DISPLAYING YOUR COLLECTION

Once you have begun to collect bottles, you will need to make some decisions about storing and displaying them. No collection is much fun if it is hidden. Gorgeous colors and forms make bottles objects you will want to display with pride.

Because glass is fragile, bottles must be protected. The ideal solution is a series of glass shelves. These may be set against windows, where they will get natural light, or they may be mounted on a wall. If you decide to put the shelves on a wall, try to have them lighted from behind.

Wood shelves are less costly than glass, but they do not display the bottles as well. Today, many collectors utilize heavy Plexiglas, which has many of the characteristics of glass.

You should fasten the bottles to the shelves. Use folded tape or sticky, puttylike clay. Fastening is especially important with historical flasks, which usually have narrow, uneven oval bases. Bottles with wide, sturdy bases can fall over, too, if the shelf is jarred.

You can display bottles in other ways. Put small ones in the boxlike area beneath a glass-top coffee table. Candy containers and figural perfume or cologne bottles are good choices for such display. Black glass looks especially attractive in an antique corner cupboard or against a white mantel.

Regardless of the display method you choose, try to maintain moderate and relatively constant temperature and humidity.

STORING BOTTLES

Many collectors find that they must store at least part of their collections. You can stack bottles in

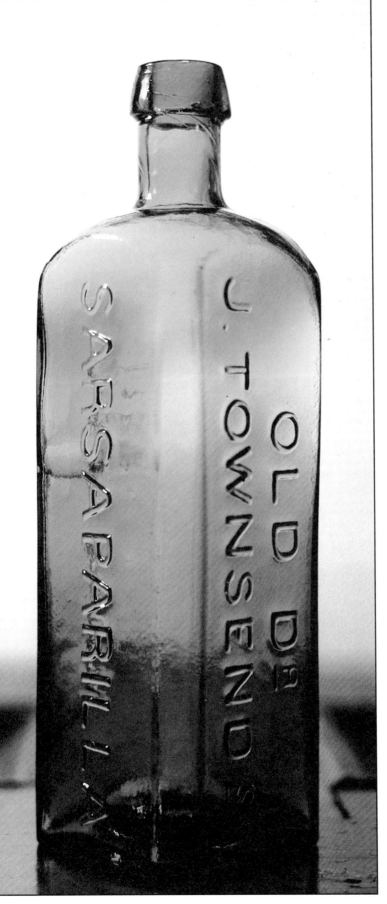

cupboards, but it is much better to store them in boxes. The best boxes for storage are cardboard or wood liquor cartons that are divided into sections. Put one bottle in each section.

Wrap the bottle in a protective material before putting it in the carton. Bubble pack and disposable diapers are excellent materials to use. Wrapping bottles and placing them in cartons is also an ideal way to prepare them for transport.

Remember that prolonged exposure to moisture can seriously damage bottles. They should never be stored in damp places.

CLEANING AND REPAIRING BOTTLES

Clean most bottles with warm water and a mild detergent. Fill the bottle, let it sit awhile, then swirl the detergent around a few times. Rinse the bottle with clear, warm water. If a stain is still visible, add a little bleach or ammonia to the water. Remove persistent, exterior stains by rubbing them gently with fine-grade steel wool soaked in water.

Hard Contents—You will probably encounter bottles in which the original contents have turned hard or gummy. These can present problems. Try cleaning the inside of the bottle with a clean toothbrush or baby-bottle brush. Some collectors add bird gravel or BB shot to detergent and water, then swirl this around in the bottle. Be sure not to use anything that will scratch or crack the inside of the bottle.

Whitish Areas—Some bottles have whitish or iridescent areas that cannot be removed. These are caused by a chemical change in the glass, resulting from long exposure to water or damp conditions. Some people find this attribute attractive; most do not. The best way to disguise this effect is to oil the interior. Home-dusting liquids, such as Endust or acrylic floor waxes, can be used for this. As long as the oil remains moist, this defect in the glass will not be visible. Of course, you should not sell or trade a bottle that has been treated in this way without informing the buyer.

Cracks and Breaks—Cracked or chipped bottles are worth far less than bottles in good condition. The worse the damage, the less valuable the piece. Repairing glass is very complex work. It involves grinding down rough edges, and using epoxies and other materials to replace missing pieces. When a bottle is repaired properly, it can appear in perfect condition.

If you plan to purchase expensive bottles, such as historical flasks, you should first purchase a long-wave black light. Instead of visible light, it produces ultraviolet (UV) radiation. When the UV strikes a piece of glass, repaired areas look different from the original material. Most black lights cost less than $50. They are a valuable detector of hidden repairs.

Start your research with the information on the bottle. Look up any embossed words in a bottle collectors' handbook. You could also check old newspapers for ads displaying similar bottles.

Gravel or BB-shot, added to detergent and water and gently swirled around in the bottle, will help clean the inside. You may also need to use a small toothbrush or baby-bottle brush.

Remember that bottles are extremely fragile. Wrap them carefully if you have to store or transport them.

BOTTLE RESEARCH

Part of the joy of collecting bottles is learning about them. Who made them? Where were they made? What purpose did they originally serve? How old are they?

Finding out about these matters takes time and effort. Books such as this one provide a good start. Information about certain popular types of bottles, such as fruit jars and historical flasks, is fairly easy to find. Information about less-popular types, such as milk, beer or food bottles, is more difficult to come by. This research can be fun, however, and great satisfaction results from learning something new.

Research methods vary according to the circumstances. Here are some general hints.

Determine the kind of bottle you are dealing with. What does the label or the embossed writing on it say? The name or advertising on the bottle will usually tell you what type of container it is. Frequently the label or embossing will tell you who manufactured the bottle contents, and where that firm was located. It is very hard to learn much about a plain, unmarked bottle.

Books—Let's assume that you have a bitters bottle. Read the books available on bitters bottles to learn about the general purpose of these containers and to find out something about the most popular brands. This general research will tell you a great deal and may even enable you to identify your bottle.

In many cases, however, books will contain little or no information about the particular bottle you are interested in. At this point, the real fun begins!

Ask Experts—Using the names and locations indicated on your bottle, write to historical societies and museums near the places where the bottle or its contents was made. Ask for any information they might have about the bottle. Be sure to include everything you know about the container. This will help focus the research efforts of the people you have written to. Always enclose a stamped, self-addressed envelope.

Directories—You can also do additional research yourself. During the 19th and early 20th centuries, most cities published directories that listed businesses and individuals. Go to the library and look through the directory of the area where the bottle or contents was manufactured. You may be able to find out which company made it, and when. If you are lucky, you may even find an advertisement for it! Such advertisements were often included in business directories.

Other sources of information include census records and old newspapers. Newspapers often included advertisements for patent medicines, canning jars and whiskeys.

Once you have gathered all the information you can, you should organize it and preserve it. Such a history is both interesting and valuable. Bottles with documented histories have greater appeal to collectors and bring higher prices.

ORGANIZING YOUR COLLECTION

The best and simplest way to organize your collection is to give each bottle a number or a letter, or both. On the bottom of each bottle, put a label with the appropriate identifying code. Write the code in a record book, along with a description of the bottle and information about when and where you found or bought it. Make note of the price you paid. This will be important if you later decide to sell the bottle.

Also include any information you have about the manufacturer and of the bottle contents, and the bottle's history or use. Once you set up this system, you will be able to quickly identify any piece in your collection by looking at the code number and then referring to the book.

Photographing Your Bottles—Some people like to photograph each bottle in their collection. If you do this, mark each slide or print with the bottle's identifying code. If possible, store the photographs with your record book.

Insurance Considerations—A system comprising a record book and photographs can be very useful, particularly for insurance purposes. More collectors are now insuring valuable bottles against theft, fire and other disasters. Many insurance companies request a photograph of each bottle. Even if the company doesn't require it, such a photograph will be helpful if you later file a claim.

If you decide to insure part of your collection, your insurer will probably require an *appraisal,* or estimate of value. Any professional bottle dealer or auctioneer can do this for you for a fee. Keep one copy of the appraisal with your records. Send another to the insurance company.

Work or Fun?—All of this may seem a great deal of effort, but to the enthusiast it's fun rather than work. Collectors who research, photograph and study their bottles appreciate them more. The bottles become more than a group of glass objects. Every bottle has its own story. As you research each one, you will also learn more about history.

In addition, you will learn about the growth and development of the bottle industry. As you become a more knowledgeable collector, you will make better finds and purchases. You will know where to go and what to look for. Luck plays a part in collecting, but in the long run the wisest collector usually turns out to be the luckiest.

Keeping a record book will help you organize your collection and will add to your enjoyment.

BOTTLE COLLECTOR'S RECORD BOOK

CODE # _____

TYPE OF BOTTLE _____

DATE OF PURCHASE _____

CONDITION _____

PURCHASE PRICE _____

ASSESSED VALUE _____

SOURCE OF ACQUISITION _____

_____

MANUFACTURER (IF KNOWN) _____

ORIGINAL CONTENTS OR USE _____

_____

DESCRIPTION

SIZE _____

COLOR _____

SHAPE _____

LABEL _____

DISTINGUISHING MARKS _____

_____

RESEARCH

PUBLICATIONS OR EXPERTS CONSULTED _____

_____

_____

RESULTS OF RESEARCH _____

_____

_____

NOTES _____

_____

_____

Price Guide

As a bottle collector, you will want to know the value of the bottles you buy and sell. Because thousands of transactions take place each month, it's important to have a price guide such as the one in this book. Remember that prices in any price guide are only *indications* of value. Actual prices asked for bottles, like those asked for other collectibles, fluctuate according to circumstances.

Here's why: Bottles are not commodities like shoes or loaves of bread. If you sell a historical flask, you cannot just call up a wholesaler and order one or two identical specimens. It may take you months or years to find a similar one. If you do, you will probably pay a different price than you paid for the one just sold. There are no fixed prices in the bottle world.

ABOUT DEALERS

Dealers price bottles based on what they originally paid for them plus business expenses and expected profit margins. For example, a dealer may have had to repair a bottle. If he did, he will pass that cost on to you. He also has to pay for overhead expenses, including advertising, shop rent and show-booth costs. A dealer will also want to make a reasonable profit. The key factor is cost. If a dealer buys a bottle at a price below market value, he may pass some of that benefit to you.

Don't be surprised if you find similar bottles selling at different prices. Prices for identical bottles in similar condition may vary as much as 15% to 25%. Bottles sold at the same time and in the same area are rarely the same price. It pays to shop around!

ABOUT THIS PRICE GUIDE

Because bottle prices vary, price guides that give single specific prices are not very helpful. This guide gives a range for each bottle, such as $10 to $15. If you come across an example similar to a bottle illustrated, its price should fall somewhere within the range given.

Condition—As mentioned, the condition of a bottle affects price. Chips and cracks are unacceptable to most knowledgeable collectors. Unless a bottle is very rare, a collector is not likely to buy a damaged one. Chips or cracks can reduce the price of a bottle by 30% to 80%, depending on the extent of the damage. Missing pieces, jagged edges and large, obvious cracks are the most serious problems. Some collectors won't accept even the tiniest hairline crack.

Price ranges given here are for bottles in good condition, with no chips or cracks.

Examining—Before you buy a bottle, carefully examine it. Look for damage. If the bottle is damaged, check whether the price has been reduced proportionately.

Glass repair has become sophisticated, so look for traces of hidden repair. You should always be suspicious of a rare, valuable piece priced below market value. Even if it appears to be in excellent condition, it may have been repaired. Be sure to check pieces for damage under an ultraviolet light.

Local Considerations—Local demand affects price. Many collectors seek bottles whose contents were made in their area and will pay a premium for such examples. You should always expect to pay more for a local product. For example, Warner patent-medicine bottles bring more in the Rochester, New York, area—where their contents were manufactured—than anywhere else.

Use this price guide to help you evaluate the bottles you own or wish to purchase. Remember that this is *only* a guide. The price you pay for a bottle will be the result of the many factors discussed here. If you understand these factors and use this guide for reference, your hobby should be both enjoyable and affordable.

ESTABLISHING PRICE RANGES

Price ranges are easier to create for some bottles than for others. The more often a specific type of bottle changes hands, the easier it is to establish a value for it. For example, patent-medicine bottles and beer bottles were produced in great quantities from 1870 to 1920. Thousands are now available regularly at shows and auctions. Prices for these bottles, in good condition, have stabilized.

The situation is different with hard-to-find bottles. For example, only six or seven examples of some types of bitters bottles are known to exist. One of these bottles rarely comes on the market. Such pieces are usually sold at auction or privately, between collectors. The price usually reflects how much the purchaser wants the piece and what he can afford to pay. The next time a similar bottle comes on the market, the selling price is not likely to be the same. In fact, the price may vary by hundreds or thousands of dollars.

Generally, prices higher than $1,000 fluctuate greatly. This is important to remember, not only in buying, but in selling. Let's say you buy a Warner's Safe Kidney and Liver Cure bottle for $12. You can be fairly certain that you can get about the same price next year from another collector. You cannot be so sure of this with a $3,000 historical flask. You may be able to get more—or you may get substantially less.

AUCTIONS

The instability of prices is especially evident at bottle auctions. Some people think auction prices are the best indication of bottle values. The truth is that auction prices are seldom realistic. A major bottle auction usually involves the sale of an important collection. Dealers and collectors come to acquire a piece from the collection. The prices may exceed those you would expect to pay a dealer for comparable bottles. Personal rivalries among collectors and dealers and "auction fever" tend to create unrealistic prices.

But don't let this keep you from attending auctions. Sometimes a small number of bottles will be offered as part of a general auction. Such an auction rarely attracts major bottle dealers or collectors. The bottles involved may sell for a fraction of their true value.

Amber patent-medicine bottles from about 1860 to 1900. Left to right: Spark's Perfect Health for Kidney & Liver Diseases, $80 to $110; Miner's Damiana and Celery Compound, $50 to $65; French's Kidney & Liver Dropsy Cure, $12 to $18; Baker's Vegetable Blood & Liver Cure, $260 to $300.

Patent-medicine bottles from about 1845 to 1885. Left to right: amber Warner's Safe Diabetes Cure, $30 to $40; pale-blue Wynkoop's Katharismic Sarsaparilla, with iron-pontil mark, $120 to $160; Dr. Sanford's Liver Invigorator, $35 to $45; green Lydia E. Pinkham's Vegetable Compound, $200 to $240.

Patent-medicine bottles with pontil marks from about 1835 to 1850. Left to right: C. W. Merchant, Chemist, $90 to $110; Alterative Syrup, $190 to $215; W. C. Sweet's King of Oils, $120 to $150; Bartine's Lotion, $65 to $90.

Patent-medicine bottles with original labels from about 1845 to 1885. Left to right: aqua Dr. Fitch's Anti-Mucus Mixture, with pontil mark, $65 to $90; amber Park's Sure Cure for the Liver and Kidneys, $20 to $40; aqua Clark Stanley's Snake Oil Liniment, $25 to $45.

Barrel-shaped bitters bottles from about 1860 to 1880. Left to right: aqua Original Pocahontas Bitters, $1,500 to $1,700; amber Hall's Bitters, $100 to $125; green Greeley's Bourbon Bitters, $300 to $400; blue unmarked barrel bitters, $324 to $450; aqua Old Sachem Bitters and Wigwam Tonic, $350 to $425. Barrel-shaped bitters are extremely popular with collectors.

Log Cabin-type bitters from about 1860 to 1880. Left to right: amber Lovegood's Family Bitters, $750 to $900; green 1860 Plantation Bitters, $350 to $425; green Kelly's Old Cabin Bitters, $325 to $450; amber American Life Bitters, $375 to $450.

Labeled bitters bottles from about 1850 to 1900. Left to right: aqua Vegetable Bilious Bitters, $30 to $45; amber Baker's Orange Grove Bitters, $140 to $160; amber Doyle's Hop Bitters, $60 to $75; aqua Gates' Life of Man Bitters, $45 to $60.

Figural bitters bottles from about 1865 to 1885. Left to right: green The Fish Bitters, $1,500 to $1,750; amber McKeever's Army Bitters, $1,900 to $2,800; amber corncob-shaped National Bitters, $185 to $225; green Brown's Celebrated Indian Herb Bitters, $900 to $1,200.

Mason's Patent canning jars from about 1870 to 1890. Left to right: pint with
Maltese cross, $4 to $5; pink Mason's Improved, with initials *C. F. J. Co.,* $6 to
$9; Two-quart Mason's Improved, with initials *C. F. J. Co.,* and on reverse,
Clyde, N.Y., $9 to $12; quart *Mason's Patent, Nov 30th 1858,* $3 to $4.

Early canning jars with unusual closures from about 1850 to 1870. Left to
right: wax sealer, N. Osborn, Rochester, N.Y., $225 to $275; Belle, $175 to
$235; Van Vliet jar, $450 to $500; Hatell's Air Tight, $140 to $165.

Figural food containers from about 1870 to 1920. Left to right: Western Spice Mills pepper sauce, $75 to $100; carnival glass syrup, $150 to $190; aqua pepper sauce, $40 to $55.

Cathedral-type pickle jars from about 1850 to 1870. Left to right: teal blue, $175 to $240; green, $80 to $110; green, $120 to $160.

Figural candy containers from about 1910 to 1930. Left to right: milk-glass clock, $55 to $70; Milk-glass suitcase, $28 to $40; gilded rabbit, $18 to $25; painted car with tin roof, $45 to $60.

Soda bottles from about 1900 to 1925. Left to right: Pepsi-Cola, Greenville, S.C., $18 to $27; Hire's Root Beer, $10 to $15; Coca-Cola, Cincinnati, Ohio, $25 to $32; Moxie, $9 to $13.

Mineral-water bottles from about 1850 to 1880. Left to right: Avon Spring Water, $80 to $100; High Rock Congress Spring, $55 to $70; Byron Acid Spring Water, $70 to $90; D. A. Knowlton, Saratoga, N.Y., $100 to $150.

Acid-etched, Coca Cola soda-fountain-dispenser
bottle from about 1920: $70 to $85.

Soda-water bottles with pontil marks, from
about 1830 to 1850. Left to right: William W.
Palleus, Premium Soda or Mineral Waters,
$70 to $100; Seymour & Knickerbocker
Mineral Water, $60 to $80; Luke Beard, $35
to $40.

Historical flasks, mid-19th century. Left to right: green, with George Washington, eagle on reverse, and pontil mark, $350 to $450; amber, with Lafayette, Liberty cap on reverse, and pontil mark, $450 to $525; dark amber, with Byron, Sir Walter Scott on reverse, $140 to $190; blue, with George Washington, Gen. Zachary Taylor on reverse, $600 to $750.

Figural flasks, mid-19th century. Left to right: blue Success to the Railroad, with railroad car and pontil mark, $1,700 to $2,100; pale-green Flora Temple, $500 to $650; amber summer-winter, $350 to $425.

Plain whiskey flasks from about 1850 to 1900. Left: amber, with illegible embossing, $7 to $9. Right: amber, embossed *Clyde Glassworks, N.Y.,* $20 to $25.

Handled whiskey jugs from about 1840 to 1870. Left to right: Star Whiskey, $140 to $180; W. Wharton's Chestnut Grove, $90 to $135; A. M. Bininger & Co., handled urn, $850 to $950; R. B. Cutter's Pure Bourbon, $250 to $300. Handled whiskey bottles are expensive, especially unusual forms such as the Bininger urn.

Wine bottles from about 1820 to 1860. Left to right: Dr. Faust's German Aromatic Wine, $60 to $90; plain amber, with pontil mark, $25 to $40; large, amber, with pontil mark, $90 to $130.

Calabash figural flasks from about 1850 to 1860. Left to right: green, with Louis Kossuth, steam frigate *Mississippi* on reverse, pontil mark, $800 to $900; amber, with hunter, fisherman on reverse, $300 to $350; blue, with Jenny Lind, glasshouse on reverse, and pontil mark, $1,000 to $1,200.

Figural whiskey bottles from about 1850 to 1880. Left to right: Old Continental
Whiskey, with embossed soldier, $1,100 to $1,250; urn-shaped A. M. Bininger
& Co., $650 to $750; barrel-shaped Chicago Whiskey, $90 to $130; Mohawk
Whiskey in form of an Indian princess, $1,400 to $1,700.

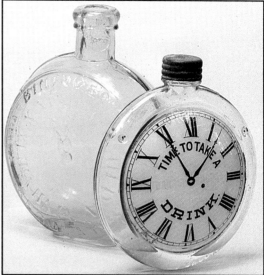

Clock-form figural whiskey bottles from about
1860 to 1900. Left to right: amber Bininger's
Regulator, $225 to $275; Dingen's Napoleon
Cocktail Bitters, $750 to $900; aqua, Bininger's
Regulator, with pontil mark, $240 to $300;
Time-To-Take-A- Drink flask, $75 to $100.

Miniature whiskey flasks from about 1870 to 1880. Top left: Bininger's Traveler's Guide, $60 to $85. Top right: Picnic, $25 to $40. Bottom left: blue clamshell, $90 to $130. Bottom right: amber clamshell, $50 to $75.

Chestnut bottles, New England, from about 1790 to 1850. Used primarily for whiskey, these free-blown bottles are usually pontil-marked and range from pale aqua to dark green.

Cone-shaped ink bottles in colors ranging from clear to dark blue from about 1870 to 1920. Prices vary from $3 to $25 for most examples. Dark blue bottles are $40 to $65.

Ink bottles in various shapes from about 1820 to 1860. Left to right: blue Harrison's Columbian Ink, $200 to $250; blue umbrella ink, with pontil mark, $150 to $190; aqua, $100 to $150; geometric form, with pontil mark, $90 to $130.

Figurals from distillers are currently becoming very popular among collectors. Left to right: Jim Beam elephant, 1960, $30 to $45; Ezra Brooks golden bear, $20 to $30.

Ink bottles in various shapes from about 1830 to 1870. Left to right: blue-green cone type, $20 to $25; Harrison's Columbian Ink, with pontil mark, $35 to $50; amber Bertinguitot, $155 to $190; aqua A. B. Tallman, $50 to $75; light-amber umbrella type, $60 to $80; black-glass umbrella type, with pontil mark, $145 to $170.

Barber bottles from about 1870 to 1910. Left to right: cobalt blue, with enamel decoration, $60 to $85; purple, with decoration and word *Vegederma* in white, $90 to $115; blue, with Mary Gregory-type decoration, $75 to $110.

Hair-tonic bottles from about 1870 to 1900. Left to right: deep-green Hall's Hair Restorer, $45 to $60; clear Burt's Hair Reviver, $10 to $15; amber John Hart & Co., $75 to $90; amber labeled Warner's Log Cabin Hair Tonic, $90 to $120.

Figural cologne bottles in clear glass from about 1870 to 1900. Left to right: crying baby, $90 to $115; baby in crib, $80 to $100; young woman with muff, $45 to $50; jester, $45 to $60.

Target balls from about 1870 to 1890. Left to right: light-blue, $60 to $75;
amber, Ira Paine's Filled Ball, Pat. Oct 23, 1877, $70 to $90; green, with figure
of man shooting gun, $75 to $100; yellow-green, $45 to $60; deep blue, with
Paine embossing, $90 to $120; green, $35 to $50.

Fire-extinguisher bottles, from about 1870 to 1890. Left to right: amber Magic
Fire Extinguisher, $45 to $65; blue Hardin's Improved Hand-Grenade Fire
Extinguisher, $75 to $95; aqua Little Giant Automatic Fire Extinguisher, $50 to
$65.

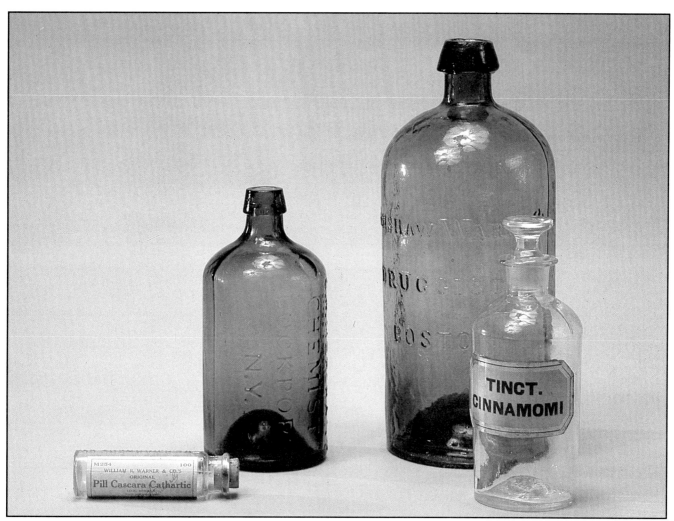

Druggists' bottles from about 1845 to 1880. Left to right: aqua, Pill Cascara Cathartic, $10 to $17; green, C. W. Merchant, Chemist, $80 to $95; green, Henshaw, Ward & Co. Druggists, with pontil mark, $200 to $250; clear, Tinct. (tincture) Cinnamomi, $45 to $55.

Bibliography

This recommended list of books can help when you do bottle research. Books marked with * are out of print and probably won't be readily available at bookstores. Books marked with † are privately printed or published by small, regional publishers. These too may be difficult to find. Therefore, you should supplement this list with books available from local libraries or used bookstores.

* Adams, John P. *Bottle Collecting in New England.* Somersworth, NH: New Hampshire Printing Co., 1969.

† Bartholomew, Edward. *1001 Bitters Bottles.* Fort Davis, TX: Bartholomew House, 1970.

Blumenstein, Lynn. *Redigging the West.* Salem, OR: Old Time Bottle Publishing Co., 1965.

* Carson, Gerald. *One for a Man, Two for a Horse.* Garden City, NY: Doubleday & Co., 1961.

† Creswick, Alice. *The Red Book of Fruit Jars.* Grand Rapids, MI: privately printed, 1970.

* Creswick, Alice, and Rodriguez, Arleta. *From Great Aunt May's Cellar—A Collection of Yesterday's Fruit Jars.* Salem, OR: Old Time Bottle Publishing Co., 1967.

† Ferraro, Pat and Bob. *A Bottle Collector's Book.* Lovelock, NV: Western Printing & Publishing Co., 1964.

† Fike, Richard E. *Handbook for the Bottle-Ologist.* Ogden, UT: privately printed, 1965.

† Gardner, Charles B., and Edwards, J. Edmund. *Price Guide to Historical Bottles and Flasks.* Stratford, CT: privately printed, 1970.

* Goodell, Donald. *The American Bottle Collector's Price Guide.* Rutland, VT: Charles E. Tuttle Co., 1974.

* Holbrook, Stewart. *The Golden Age of Quackery.* New York: The Macmillan Co., 1959.

* Kendrick, Grace. *The Antique Bottle Collector.* Ann Arbor, MI: Edwards Brothers, 1963.

* Kendrick, Grace. *The Mouth-Blown Bottle.* Ann Arbor, MI: Edwards Brothers, 1968.

* Ketchum, William C., Jr. *A Treasury of American Bottles.* New York, NY: Bobbs-Merrill, 1975.

* Knittle, Rhea Mansfield. *Early American Glass.* New York, NY: The Century Co., 1927.

Kovel, Ralph and Terry. *The Kovel's Bottle Price List.* New York, NY: Crown Publishers, 1982.

McKearin, George S. and Helen. *American Glass.* New York, NY: Crown Publishers, 1950.

McKearin, Helen, and Wilson, Kenneth. *American Bottles and Flasks and Their Ancestry.* New York, NY: Crown Publishers, 1978.

* Maust, Don. *Bottle and Glass Handbook.* Uniontown, PA. E. G. Warman Publishing Co., 1956.

Munsey, Cecil. *The Illustrated Guide to Collecting Bottles.* New York, NY: Hawthorn Books, 1970.

* Reed, Adele. *Bottle Talk.* Bishop, CA: Chalfant Press, 1961.

† Ring, Carlyn. *For Bitters Only.* Boston, MA: Nimrod Press, 1980.

* Sellari, Dot and Carol. *Official Guide to Bottles, New and Old.* Florence, AL: House of Collectibles, 1977.

* Thompson, James H. *Bitters Bottles.* Watkins Glen, NY: Century House, 1946.

Tibbitts, John G. *John Doe Bottle Collector.* Santa Cruz, CA: Heirloom Press, 1967.

* Toulouse, Julian Harrison. *Bottle Makers and Their Marks.* Camden, NJ: Thomas Nelson, 1971.

† Umberger, Art and Jewel. *It's a Bitters.* Tyler, TX: Corker Book Co., 1967.

* Van Rensselaer, Stephen. *Early American Bottles and Flasks.* Parts I and II. Peterborough, NH: Transcript Publishing Co., 1926.

† Wagoner, George. *Restoring Old Bottles.* West Sacramento, CA: privately printed, 1966.

* Watkins, Laura Woodside. *American Glass and Glassmaking.* New York, NY: Chanticleer Press, 1950.

* Watson, Richard. *Bitters Bottles.* New York, NY: Thomas Nelson & Sons, 1965.

† Wilson, Bill and Betty. *19th Century Medicine in Glass.* Amador City, CA: 19th Century Hobby and Publishing Co., 1971.

* Wilson, Kenneth M. *New England Glass and Glassmaking.* New York, NY: Thomas Y. Crowell Co., 1972.

* Yount, John T. *Bottle Collector's Handbook and Pricing Guide.* San Angelo, TX: Educator Books, 1970.

Index